CONTENTS

P9-BXV-447

CHRISTMAS COMES BUT ONCE A YEAR...

Christmas is a wonderful time, when our homes are filled with a sense of magic and rising excitement, and laden with the enticing aromas of sweets and spices. This is a time to give ourselves a few days of warmth and celebration in the midst of winter. There is a great sense of occasion that is sorely needed to help us through these cold, dark days. Christmas encourages friends and family to come together, baking cakes and making decorations. Christmas is a time to appreciate the joy of life, our health, our friends and our family. The beautiful projects in this book will help you make this special time of year extra-special.

But beware! The pressure of trying to create the perfect Christmas may also mean that we set our ambitions too high. Don't wear yourself out – just do as much as you can manage. Don't be afraid to drop some projects so that you have more time to enjoy the ones you really want to make. The projects you don't get around to this year you can always try out next year, or the year after... If you place too many demands on yourself you might just end up exhausted by the time Christmas is over.

Make less of the big events, and instead enjoy the cosy little happenings that turn up along the way. Make the best of these occasions, because you deserve some happy, relaxed times in the middle of all the stress that Christmas can bring.

Here are some wonderful projects for you to try out this Christmas...

This book features projects for accessories, decorations, toys and home furnishings, many of which make excellent Christmas presents. We also aim to show how the patterns you sew can be used in your home. If your colour scheme or your personal style is different, just remember that it's the patterns that count – they can be interpreted in many ways.

Have a great Christmas!

Tone Finnanger

MT. PLEASANT PUBLIC LIBRARY
MT. PLEASANT, IOWA

DISCARDED

Sew Pretty
Christmas Homestyle

Over 35
irresistible
projects to
fall in love
with

David and Charles

A DAVID & CHARLES BOOK

Copyright © J.W. Cappelens
Forlag, AS 2007
Cappelen Hobby
www.cappelen.no/hobby
Originally published in Norway
as *Tildas julehus*

First published in the UK in 2008
by David & Charles
David & Charles is an F+W
Publications Inc. company
4700 East Galbraith Road
Cincinnati, OH 45236
Reprinted 2008 (twice)

All rights reserved. No part of this
publication may be reproduced,
stored in a retrieval system, or
transmitted, in any form or by any
means, electronic or mechanical,
by photocopying, recording
or otherwise, without prior
permission in writing from the
publisher.

The designs and projects in this
book are copyright and must not
be made for resale.

A catalogue record for this book is
available from the British Library.

ISBN-13: 978-0-7153-2961-0
paperback
ISBN-10: 0-7153-2961-8
paperback

Printed in China by Donnelley
for David & Charles
Brunel House   Newton Abbot
Devon

Visit our website at
www.davidandcharles.co.uk

David & Charles books are
available from all good bookshops;
alternatively you can contact our
Orderline on 0870 9908222 or
write to us at FREEPOST EX2
110, D&C Direct, Newton Abbot,
TQ12 4ZZ (no stamp required
UK only); US customers call
800-289-0963 and Canadian
customers call 800-840-5220.

FABRICS AND MATERIALS

FABRICS

In this book I have mostly used patterned and self-coloured materials and woollen felt. In addition I have used classic striped and checked materials, of which many variations can be found in quilting shops. The bodies of figures are sewn from flesh-coloured fabrics, while the pigs and geese (pages 44–49) are made from sand-coloured and white material.

SPECIAL MATERIALS

Many of the projects require you to use a fibre felt material with adhesive on one side that produces a padded, slightly stiffened result. Fibre felt can be quilted, as seen in some of the projects in the book, although it doesn't produce a particularly ruffled quilt effect.

Thin, stiff fibre felt with adhesive on one side can be used to stiffen items such as hats, gift bags and so on.

If you only want to reinforce a thin material without stiffening, you can use a thinner, softer type of fibre felt.

For appliqué projects, use a specialist paper with an adhesive side that is pressed against the reverse side of material with an iron; the paper is then torn off, resulting in an adhesive material for simple appliqué work. This is used here to attach the faces to the babushka dolls (pages 98–99).

MISCELLANEOUS

Tape, jewels, buttons, hair, paper and paper decorations, small coat hangers, haloes and so on are available from all good haberdashery stores.

Under 'Acknowledgments' on pages 132–133 we have listed the suppliers who provided furniture and other items for the photographs in this book.

TECHNIQUES

YO-YOS

Yo-yos are cloth circles that are gathered to form smaller circles, making pretty decorations for the projects in this book. This a project that you can make while relaxing in your armchair.

For the smallest yo-yos, which are used, among other things, for the rings on page 93, cut a circle of about 6cm (2½in) diameter plus seam allowance. A variety of different-sized lids, bowls and saucers were used to draw larger circles, the largest of which is about 15cm (6in) in diameter. When the yo-yo is finished it will be about half as large as the original circle.

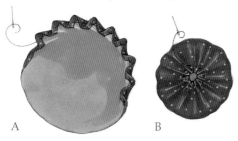

A   B

Instructions

Draw a circle of the required size on the wrong side of the material and add a seam allowance when you cut it out. Fold the seam allowance inwards around the edge and sew stitches at regular intervals through the circle and the seam allowance, as in Figure A. The stitches should be from 0.5cm (¼in) long for the smallest circles to about 1cm (½in) for the largest. If you make the stitches too small, it may be difficult to gather the yo-yo together.

When you have sewn all the way round the circle, gather it tightly together. Afterwards, it is a good idea to sew round once more through the folds a little further from the centre so as to gather it tightly, as shown in Figure B. Tie off the thread.

Attach the yo-yo to the model using invisible stitching around the edge.

Yo-yos to be used as Christmas tree decorations are made by cutting a cardboard circle half as large as the cloth circle without seam allowance and before gathering. Gather the cloth circle around the card circle and then sew buttonhole stitch with embroidery yarn around the edge through the card and cloth. Add a hanging loop of yarn before finishing off.

CIRCULAR DECORATIONS

A number of projects featured in the book are decorated with various circles in the form of yo-yos, woollen felt dots, buttons and jewels in harmonious colour combinations.

In addition, stitched circles are used that are made by folding a rose-patterned material or similar right side to right side and drawing a small circle of about 4.5cm (1¾in) diameter – just large enough to contain a rose. Sew around the edges. Cut out the circle and cut a reversing opening through one of the layers of material.

Turn the circle inside out and push the edges out using a wooden stick before ironing.

The circle can be sewn directly onto the model or attached to a larger yo-yo.

The woollen felt dots are made by cutting small circles of felt and sewing them to the model using buttonhole stitch. The stitches around the edge will make it uneven; the trick here is to hold the scissors at an angle to the edge and trim or round off the fringe so that it doesn't protrude between the stitches. Make sure you don't cut through any of the stitches.

TWIG WREATHS
You can either buy ready-made wreaths or make them yourself using slender twigs and thin, dark, steel wire. If you feel the wreath is too tidy-looking, pull out a few twigs to make it look more ragged.

Use small, transparent beads to create the appearance of frost on the twigs.

Pour the beads out onto a dinner plate. Use a glue gun to apply glue to an area of the wreath, and press the sticky side of the wreath into the beads on the plate. Add glitter to the wreath with a glitter stick or use transparent adhesive and loose glitter.

STAMPING MATERIAL
For the advent calendars in this book (pages 102–105 and 118–119), I printed the numbers using the calendar

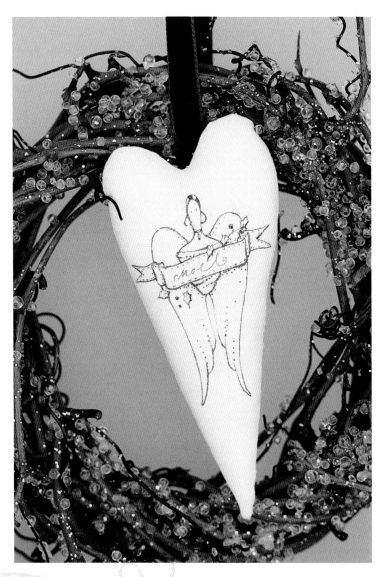

numbers from a stamp set. I have also used stamps to decorate the spice bags and hearts. Material isn't as easy to handle as flat, stiff paper, so you need to take some precautions to obtain a good result when stamping.

You should only stamp on a single layer of material, placed on a hard surface. The edges of the stamp, around the motif, will more easily mark material than paper, so cut an opening in a piece of paper, slightly larger than the stamp motif and place it over the rubber so that only

the motif protrudes. Working in this way means that the ink from the stamp pad will only cover the motif itself. Remove the paper before stamping.

Make sure you use plenty of colour when stamping textiles – if the stamp pad has been used frequently, it may only produce a faint impression on the fabric.

Test the stamp on a spare piece of cloth to find out exactly how to get the right distance between numbers, and so on, before you start work on the actual project.

STENCILS AND TRANSFERRING PATTERNS

I have a small, reasonably priced, combined printer and photocopier, which I find a really useful tool. If I want to make a stencil, I simply copy the pattern from a book on to thick card and cut the stencil out using sharp scissors. If I need to make a larger pattern, I can use the photocopier to enlarge it, and make several copies if necessary. Afterwards, all the parts can be assembled.

Before I had this machine I used to go to the library to make copies. There they only had ordinary thin paper, which I had to glue onto cardboard before I cut out the stencils.

If you want to transfer needlework details such as text for a tapestry, this can be done by holding the material, with the pattern under it, against a window so that the pattern is visible through the material. Transfer the pattern to the material using an invisible ink pen. Another possibility is to place the material on a tabletop, lay carbon paper on it and then the pattern on top. This should always be done before attaching the fibre felt, so you only have a single layer of material.

FACES

It is always best to wait until hair, hats, ears, horns and so on have been attached before making the features for a model's face. This makes it easier to see where the eyes should be located. Stick two pins into the head to check where the eyes should be. Remove the pins and fix the eyes where the pin-holes are. Use the head of a small pin dipped in black paint to mark the eyes in.

Rouge, lipstick or similar can be applied with a dry brush to make rosy cheeks.

PAINTING DETAILS

Details such as the soles of small shoes, skates, beaks, snouts and the hair on the babushka dolls are painted with water-based craft paint. Textile paint can also be used, which is especially important if a project is to be washable.

For most of the models I have used a dark brown colour, while on the dark-coloured teddy bears I have used pink and a sand colour. For the beaks of the geese I used a terracotta colour, or you could use a warm shade of brown.

Mark the area to be painted with an invisible ink pen or a thin ball-point pen and paint with a small, flat brush.

The white highlight on beaks can be applied in the same way as eyes. Use a pin with a round head on the snout of the hobby reindeer (pages 116–117) to produce a larger highlight spot.

HAIR

The hairstyle on the angels is made with the help of doll's hair and thin steel wire. The best method is to stick a long piece of steel wire right through the angel's head. You can use a large bodkin to pull the wire through, as in Figure A.

If you find this difficult, just stick a length of steel wire well in on each side of the head. Tie a long piece of doll's hair around one of the wires and twist the hair back and forth on the back and top of the head. Attach the hair evenly on the head using a needle and thread, and then twist the doll's hair about 4cm (1½in) along the wire on each side, as shown in Figure B.

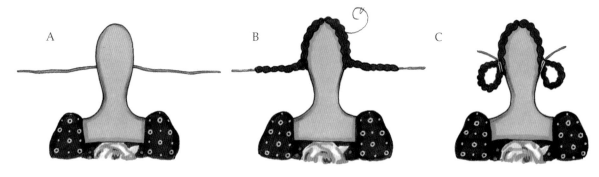

STUFFED FIGURES
STEP BY STEP

Sew

Avoid cutting out the figure beforehand unless this is necessary. Instead, fold the material double and draw the figure on it using the pattern. Mark reversing openings.

Sew along the line in the drawing. Use a stitch length of about 1.5–2mm (¹⁄₁₆in) and sew carefully, so as to avoid irregularities. See Figure A.

Cut out

Cut out the figure. The seam allowance should be narrow; 3–4mm (¹⁄₈in) is best. However, at reversing openings a wider seam allowance, about 7–8mm (¹⁄₄in), should be cut.

Cut a slit in the seam allowance where the seam curves inwards, as in Figure B.

Reverse

A flower stick is a useful tool for reversing; use mainly the blunt end, except for small details like birds' beaks, which should be carefully worked out using the sharp end of the stick. To avoid pushing the tip of the stick through the material, cut off a small section so that it is less pointed. Long, narrow parts such as angels' legs can be reversed by pushing the blunt end of the stick into the foot, as in Figure C. Begin close to the foot and pull the leg down over the wooden stick, as shown in Figure D. Continue to pull the leg down along the stick until the tip or foot emerges through the reversing opening, then grip the foot and pull, while holding the rest of the leg to reverse it, as in Figure E. Arms can, of course, be reversed in the same way.

Fold in

Fold in the extra seam allowance at openings along the seam, except on the legs and arms of angels: here the seam allowance is to be inside the body and should therefore not be folded in.

Stuffing the figure

When inserting the stuffing, use a finger where possible, and the end of a pen or pencil where your fingers don't reach. If the tool is too narrow it will simply slide through the stuffing.

Push the stuffing loosely into the figure, avoiding pressing all the stuffing together into a lump before it is in position. Press the stuffing carefully but firmly into place and add more until you have a firm and well-shaped figure.

Sew up the reversing openings.

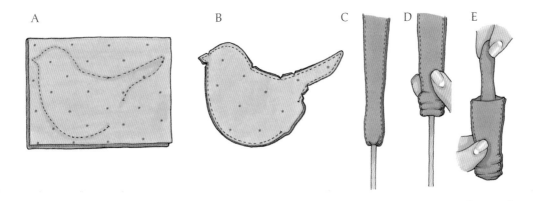

A   B   C   D   E

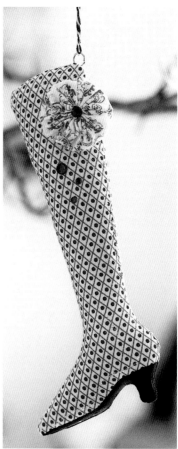

Bend the plait in underneath so that it makes a drop shape, and twist the end of the wire around the bottom end of the plait against the head, to finish off, as in Figure C. Cut off excess wire.

The plaits on the pixie girls (pages 60–62) consist of six equal lengths of doll's hair twisted together in the centre. Fix the hair at the top of the head so that three locks hang down on each side and make ordinary plaits. Tie a ribbon where you want the plaits to end and cut off the excess hair. The pixie's head will be covered by the hat and only the plaits will be visible.

The hair on the pixie boys (page 63) is made by placing a small bunch of hair over the head before attaching the hat, so that just a few curls stick out on each side.

EFFECTS

Some of the projects, such as the sand-coloured angels' wings, the pigs and the appliquéd birds, have been decorated to give a slightly worn or vintage appearance. A touch of colour has also been added to the appliquéd muffins (page 66) to give them a three-dimensional shadow effect, helping them to stand out from the background, like the appliquéd angel busts (pages 78–79).

This effect is achieved with the help of sand-coloured or brown textile stamp pads. Brush on the colour using a dry paintbrush.

Textile stamp sets with these colours are obtainable from good haberdashery stores.

A glitter stick can be used to add glitter to the finished projects if desired.

THE ENTRANCE HALL

The entrance hall is decorated with boots and skates hung on large branches in a plant pot. The small paper bags are motifs from a cut-out sheet, decorated with jewels and glitter. There are also ideas here for Christmas presents in the form of handbags, hats, mittens and scarves.

BAGS

YOU WILL NEED

Material for bag and handle

High-volume fibre felt

Material for the lining

Press stud

Ribbon for decoration if desired

The pattern is on page 152

A

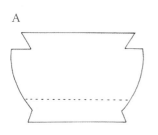

B

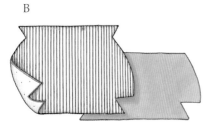

C

D

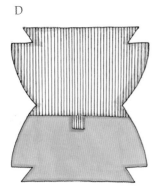

E

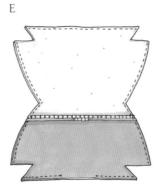

INSTRUCTIONS

Note that the pattern is divided up so it fits on the page. Put the pieces together as indicated in Figure A.

Cut two pieces of material and two pieces of high-volume fibre felt large enough for the whole pattern part and iron the fibre felt onto the wrong side of the material pieces. Cut two pieces of lining material corresponding to the pattern part as far as the dotted line. Add seam allowances to all parts as shown in Figure B.

Cut two pieces of material measuring 8×4cm (3⅛×1½in) to make press stud attachments and add a seam allowance.

Fold the seam allowance inwards on one long edge and the two short edges of each piece of material. Now fold each piece of material double to make them 4×4cm (1½×1½in), with a seam allowance at each end, as shown in Figure C, and sew up the open sides as shown in Figure D.

Place the front piece on each of the main material parts right side to right side and place the small press stud attachments between the layers in the middle of the bag part. Sew together to make two bag parts as shown in Figure E.

Attach one part of the press stud to each of the two press stud attachments as described on the packet.

Place the two bag parts right side to right side and sew around them as shown in Figure F, leaving a reversing opening in the lining.

Place the sides and the angled part to form the base to face each other and sew the sides together as shown in Figure G.

F

G

H

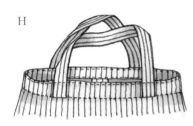

inwards on the long edges and fold the strips double to make them 4×57cm (1½×22½in) with a seam allowance at each end. Sew the open edges together.

Mark about 7cm (2¾in) in from each side at the top of the bag and place the handle with the ends pointing downwards about 2.5cm (1in) from the edge of the bag and attach them with pins.

Sew all the way round the bag about 3cm (1¼in) in from the edge, attaching the handles at the same time, as shown in Figure H. The seam will be

positioned approximately at the join between the material and lining inside the bag; make sure the press stud attachments are pointing downwards when you sew.

Iron the handles upwards and then sew a seam round the whole bag about 3mm (⅛in) from the edge, as shown in Figure I.

If you like, you can thread a velvet ribbon through the 'channels' created on each side where the handles are attached, and tie it in a bow at the front for decoration.

Cut away surplus seam allowance, turn inside out and iron the bag. The lining will now start a little way down on the inside of the bag, forming a neat edge.

Cut out two strips of material measuring 57×8cm (22½×3⅛in) for the handles, adding a seam allowance. Cut two corresponding pieces of high-volume fibre felt, but without a seam allowance.

Iron the fibre felt strips onto the wrong side of the material strips, distributing the seam allowance on the material equally on each side of the fibre felt. Fold the seam allowance

HATS

This hat is a real treasure, and a favourite of mine.
There are patterns for both small and large versions

INSTRUCTIONS

The hat can be made of woollen felt or another material, both with lining; if you use a thin material it will keep its shape better with the help of stiffening fibre felt.

The pattern is in two sizes, one for adults and one for children. Measure around the head with a tape measure to ensure that the hat will fit. The adult's hat will fit about 53–60cm (21–23½in) head size, and the child's hat about 46–52 (18–20½in). The sizes are approximate, depending on the elasticity of the fabric.

The hat pattern is cut out in one piece by placing the pattern parts edge to edge and repeating six times, to produce a wavy crown shape (see Figure A). Cut out the felt and lining to this shape, adding a seam allowance. Place the two parts right side to right side and sew along the bottom edge, as shown in Figure A.

Fold apart the lining and felt and sew all the curved edges together. Iron the seam allowances apart inside the hat before sewing up the open edge, leaving a reversing opening in the lining, as shown in Figure B. Cut off the surplus seam allowance.

Turn the hat inside out and sew up the reversing opening. Push the lining into the hat and iron the folded edge. Sew a seam along the folded edge so that the lining stays in place, as shown in Figure C.

YOU WILL NEED

Woollen felt or material
Material for the lining
Materials for decoration if desired
The pattern is on page 139

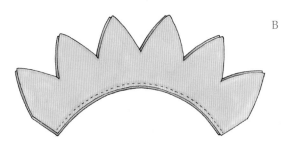

B

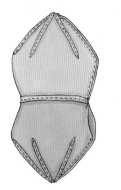

C

HAT STAND

You can make an attractive hat stand to display your hats by fixing a wooden rod into a base. Cut the rod to the desired height. Cut a circle of material about 20cm (8in) in diameter and fold the edge inwards, tacking around it, as for the yo-yos on page 8. Gather the circle slightly and stuff well with padding before threading it onto the rod and gathering tightly around the rod. Wind the thread a few times around the rod before attaching firmly.

Woollen felt mittens with a personal touch make excellent Christmas presents. They are also warm and cosy

MITTENS

YOU WILL NEED
Woollen felt
Flat elastic
Materials for decoration
The pattern is on page 135

A

B

C

INSTRUCTIONS
This pattern is in two sizes, one suitable for children and the other for adults. Place a hand on the pattern to see if the mitten will fit. If the size isn't right, use a photocopier to enlarge or reduce the pattern.

Each mitten consists of three parts: a lower part with a thumb, an upper part with a thumb and the whole mitten part. Cut out the parts, adding a seam allowance, as shown in Figure A.

Make sure you cut the upper and lower parts with the thumb mirror-imaged for each mitten to produce a left-hand and a right-hand mitten.

Place the upper and lower parts of each mitten right side to right side and sew them together as shown in Figure B.

Place the assembled part with the thumb on the whole mitten part right side to right side and sew around the edge as shown in Figure C.

Fold down the seam allowance at the top and tack together round the edge without sewing all the way through the felt. Cut off surplus seam allowance around the mitten.

Cut about 6cm (2½in) of elastic for each mitten, or 5cm (2in) for the child's size. Attach the elastic at the side where the thumb is, about where the dotted line is in the pattern. First sew the ends of the elastic firmly in place in the seam allowance on each side of the mitten. Pull the mitten onto the hand and push out so that the elastic stretches to about the width of the mitten. Tack the elastic all the way round the mitten without sewing through the felt. Reverse the mitten. The elastic will now make regular gathers on the bottom of the mitten and prevent it from falling off the hand. Decorate the mitten if desired as described on page 8.

SCARF

YOU WILL NEED

Woollen felt and material
Material for the lining
Ribbon for decoration if desired

INSTRUCTIONS

Cut a 17cm-wide (6¾in) strip
from the whole width of a
roll of woollen felt (a roll is
normally 140–150cm/55–59in
wide). Add a seam allowance
to the width of the strip.
Now sew a piece of material
measuring 17×14cm (6¾×5½in)
to each end of the felt strip,
remembering to add a seam
allowance. If desired, sew a
velvet ribbon or some other
material at the join between
the material and the felt. Cut
a piece of lining material the
size of the whole scarf; you can
also use two pieces of material
joined together. Place the scarf
and lining right side to right
side and sew around, leaving
a reversing opening. Cut away
surplus seam allowance, turn
inside out and iron the scarf,
before sewing up the reversing
opening. A pin made from
a yo-yo with a circle sewn in
the centre makes a pretty
decoration: see the yo-yos and
circle decorations on page 8.

An elegant scarf with a personal touch with matching hat and mittens – great for those cold winter days

MINIATURE BOOTS AND SKATES

YOU WILL NEED

Material

Dark brown craft paint

Zinc wire or similar, pliers and glue for making skates

Materials for decoration

Stuffing

The pattern is on page 136

INSTRUCTIONS

Fold a piece of material, that is large enough for the boot or the skate, right side to right side and sew around the edges as shown in Figure A, remembering to leave a reversing opening. Cut out, turn inside out, iron and then stuff before sewing up the reversing opening. Paint the sole with brown paint as indicated by the dotted line in the pattern; see 'Painting details' on page 10.

If you want, you can sew laces on the boots or skates using embroidery thread.

Skate blades: Bend the zinc wire into a curled tip for a blade by gripping in pliers and twisting the rest of the wire around the pliers. Cut the wire so that the blade is about the same size as that shown in the pattern.

Fix the blade to the bottom of the skate with glue, as well as tacking it with thread, as shown in Figure B.

If you like, you could decorate the boot or skate with ribbon and jewels.

A
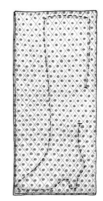

B

Keyrings shaped like boots...

What could be better to decorate the entrance hall than pretty miniature boots and skates?

THE LIVING ROOM

The Christmas living room is decorated in dark brown and pink, to give a pretty holiday atmosphere. The Christmas tree is decorated with birds, paper cones and small, painted wooden figures. Here we also find elegant, long-legged angels and babushka dolls, described on page 98, dressed in brown dresses.

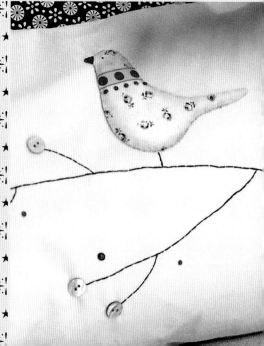

ANGELS

YOU WILL NEED
Flesh-coloured fabric
Material for dress
Material for pantaloons
Material for wings
Thin fibre felt if necessary
Stuffing
Ribbon and jewels for
necklace
Paint for shoes
Halo
Figure stand if desired

INSTRUCTIONS
The angel pattern is in two sizes. The living room angels are the small ones, about 48cm (19in) tall. The pattern for the small angels is on page 144. The large angel shown on page 131 is 80cm (31½in) tall and the pattern is on pages 148–149.

BODY
Read the section on 'Stuffed figures step by step' on page 11 before starting.

Sew together a strip of flesh-coloured fabric and a strip of dress material for the body. Iron apart the seam allowances and fold the assembled strip of material right side to right side. Draw the outline of the body so that the join between flesh fabric and dress material is roughly as indicated by the dotted line in the pattern. Sew together and fold the

flesh-coloured fabric and the material for the arms in the same way as for the body; then draw the arms.

Fold the material for the legs double and draw the legs. Sew around the parts, as shown in Figure A.

Cut out, turn inside out, iron and stuff the body and arms as described on page 11.

If you want to be able to bend the legs of the figure, first stuff half the leg, then sew a seam across before stuffing the rest, as shown in Figure B.

PANTALOONS OR TROUSERS
The pantaloons are simply made by attaching two trouser legs to the body when attaching the legs. Fold material for the trouser legs right side to right side and draw the outline. Sew around and cut out. Fold up the seam allowance at the bottom and fix with a few stitches or some fabric adhesive before turning inside out and ironing. Thread the legs into the trouser legs so that the openings are together and sew a seam across the openings to keep everything in place, as shown in Figure C.

Fold in the seam allowance around the opening on the body, insert the legs and

sew in place. Fold in the seam allowance round the openings on the arms. Place the shoulders against the openings and attach them by sewing round the openings so that the arms hang straight down beside the body as in Figure D.

SKIRT
Cut out a piece of dress material measuring 36×25cm (14×10in) and add a seam allowance. Fold the skirt double right side to right side so that it is 18cm (7in) wide and sew along the open edge. Fold the edge inwards and iron and sew a seam along the bottom edge of the skirt. Fold in the seam allowance at the top and attach the skirt in pleats around the angel, with the seam in the skirt at the back. The skirt should be attached fairly high up on the angel's body, about 2cm (¾in) from the dress edge over the bust.

WINGS
The pattern for the wings has a fold-line on it and should be twice as large as shown.

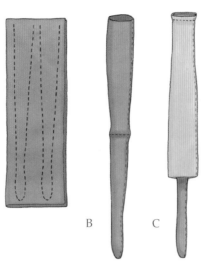

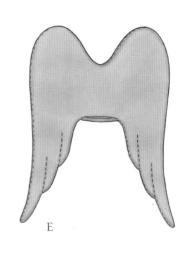

A   B   C   E

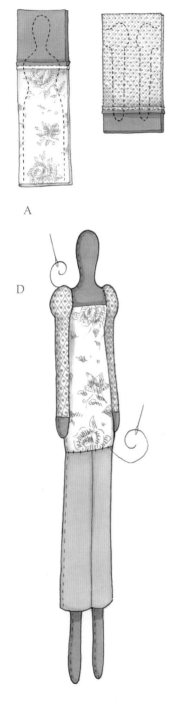

D

If desired, iron thin fibre felt onto the wrong side of the wing material for a smoother appearance and fold the material right side to right side. Draw the outline of the wings on the material and cut out.

Make sure that you cut through the seam allowance where the seam is turned inwards and turn the wings fully inside out with the help of a wooden stick.

Iron the wings and sew seams using a sewing machine a short distance up from the wing tips as indicated in the pattern, as shown in Figure E.

Stuff the channels created between the seams using a wooden stick and stuff the rest of the wings firmly before sewing up the reversing opening. Stitch the wings to the figure, using embroidery yarn and a bodkin.

If desired, attach a narrow ribbon and a jewel to make a necklace around the angel's neck. If the ribbon is too wide it can be folded double.

Make hair, face and effects as described on pages 10 and 12. Use a ready-made halo or make one out of zinc wire or similar and push it well into the head.

Paint the shoes as described on page 10. The angels have small shoes, painted as indicated by the lowest dotted line shown on the pattern.

Attach the angel to a doll stand by sharpening the end of the rod with a pencil sharpener and pushing it up into the angel until the feet are on the base of the stand. If the angel is to be hung up, sew a small ribbon loop to it.

The heart corresponds to the smallest heart pattern, as in 'Hearts' on pages 70–71.

The main patterns are on page 144 (leg and pantaloon patterns on pages 136 and 137) and pages 148–149.

BIRDS

YOU WILL NEED
Material
Brown craft paint
Materials for decoration if desired
Stuffing
The pattern is on page 137

INSTRUCTIONS
Fold a piece of material twice as large as the bird right side to right side. Draw the outline of the bird and sew around the edge, leaving a reversing opening. Cut out, turn the bird inside out and stuff as described on page 11. Sew up the reversing opening. Paint the beak with craft paint and, if desired, sew on a small metal ring for hanging.

BIRD APPLIQUÉS

In addition to the materials for the bird as above, you will need some dark brown embroidery thread and mother-of-pearl buttons to create the effect of berry-laden twigs.

Take note that there are different patterns for the stuffed birds and the appliquéd birds. Sew the appliquéd bird in the same way as the stuffed bird, but sew around the whole bird and make a reversing opening through one layer of material as indicated in the pattern. Putting a little stuffing in the appliquéd bird is effective, although a very small amount is needed. Decorate the bird with ribbon and jewels before attaching it to the background using invisible stitching around the edge.

Draw the branches freehand using an invisible ink pen and sew with embroidery yarn. I used three strands of yarn. Sew with backstitch. Sew on the mother-of-pearl buttons or similar to form berries on the branches.

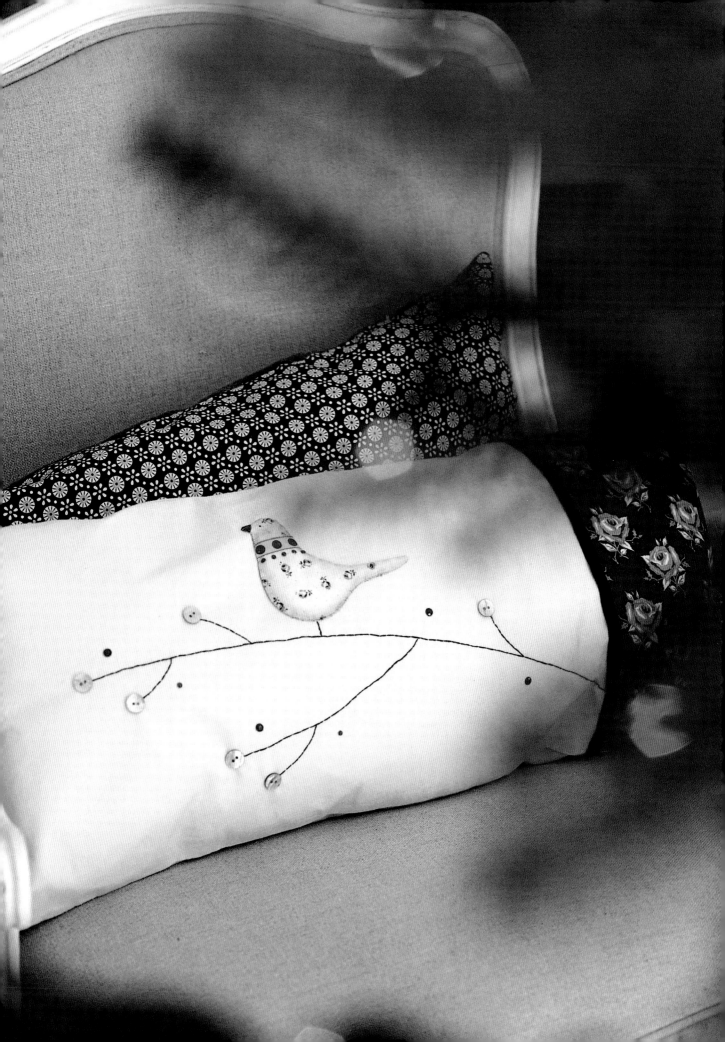

BLANKET WITH WOOLLEN FELT LINING

A cosy blanket with a woollen felt lining is lovely and warm in winter. This blanket is made from 20×20cm (8×8in) squares (with a seam allowance) sewn together. The squares are in alternating brown and patterned materials.

When you've made the blanket big enough, place it right side to right side on a piece of woollen felt of the same size. Sew around the edges, remembering to leave a reversing opening. Cut away the surplus seam allowance around the edge, turn the blanket inside out and sew up the reversing opening. Iron the whole blanket thoroughly and attach a safety pin through both layers at each point where the corners of the squares meet.

Make yourself comfortable in an armchair and sew on mother-of-pearl buttons, or similar, at the location of each safety pin, sewing the layers together before removing the safety pins.

Home-made blankets and cushions add comfort to your living room. If you line the blanket with woollen felt, it will keep you warm on cold winter evenings

CUSHIONS

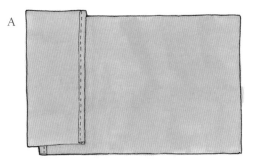

A

Cushions are a simple way of giving a room a fresh new look, and they are easy to sew. The simplest technique is to sew the back in the same way as most pillowcases, with two pieces of material that overlap. Bear in mind that if the narrow part is to be underneath at the end, it must be on top when the parts of the cover are sewn together. See Figure A.

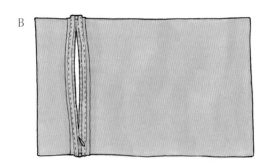

B

It is also easy to sew a zip fastener into the back, by dividing the back into two parts and sewing in the zip fastener before the front and back of the cover are sewn together. See Figure B.

If you like, you can decorate the cushions as described under 'Yo-yos' and 'Circle decorations' on page 8.

CUT-OUT PICTURES

YOU WILL NEED

Patterned paper

A figure or motif

Glue stick

Sandpaper

Sand-coloured or brown stamp pad

Medium-sized paintbrush

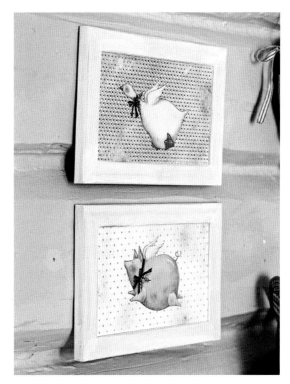

INSTRUCTIONS

Make the background by cutting patterned paper to fit the backing card of the frame. If the paper is thin it must be glued to cardboard. Rub some areas of the paper with sandpaper. Cut out and glue on the desired motif. Brush the picture with ink from the stamp pad using a paintbrush to give an antique appearance. If you like, you can paint the frame and sandpaper the edges to give a worn or vintage effect before you place the picture in the frame.

Wall tapestries made of paper with a worn effect make simple and effective decorations. Why not make your own Christmas pictures?

THE DINING ROOM

Angel pigs and geese flutter over the table and fly up to heaven.

Branches balance precariously in the chandelier, lending

a dramatic atmosphere to a festive Christmas meal.

Menus and place cards tell guests where they should

sit and what they are about to eat.

ANGEL PIGS

YOU WILL NEED
Sand-coloured material

Thin fibre felt

White material

Stuffing

Zinc wire or similar for the tail

Halo

Velvet ribbon and red berries or similar for de-coration

Flower sticks to support the seated pig

The patterns are on pages 138 and 140

INSTRUCTIONS
Note that the pig pattern is in two sizes; the larger one is divided up into two pieces to fit the page, but is assembled in the same way as the small one.

Read the section 'Stuffed figures step by step' on page 11 before starting.

Cut out a piece of material twice as large as the body and iron an equally large piece of thin fibre felt onto the wrong side. The fibre felt will reinforce the material and give the body of the pig a smoother appearance.

Fold in two a piece of material large enough for four legs and two ears; here it is not necessary to

add any reinforcement. Draw the outline of all the parts on the material and sew around them. Note the openings indicated by dotted lines in the pattern, as shown in Figure A.

Cut out the parts and turn them inside out. Turn the body and ears inside out through the reversing opening and cut openings in the legs through one material layer, as indicated in the pattern.

Iron all the parts and stuff the body and legs.

If the pig is to be sitting, the front legs must be reinforced so as to bear the weight of the body. Cut a piece of a flower stick slightly shorter than the leg and push it into the leg through the reversing opening after the leg has been stuffed.

Stitch the reversing openings in the legs closed and attach the legs to the figure with pins so that you can position them correctly before sewing them on. On the sitting pig it is important that the legs be positioned so that the pig keeps its balance.

Fold in the seam allowance on the ears, fold the ears slightly and tack them in place. Attach a thread behind one ear and sew through the head with a bodkin to make a stitch across the snout. Sew back through the head and tighten slightly before tying off the thread as shown in Figure B.

A

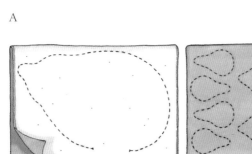

B

C

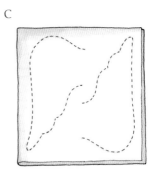

Maybe the pigs are a little naughty,
but I think they are rather splendid,
with their wings decorated with a
sprinkling of glitter

WINGS

Fold a piece of material twice as large as two wings right side to right side. Trace and sew around the wings, as in Figure C.

Cut out, turn inside out and iron the wings. Sew seams on the wings using a sewing machine, as indicated in the pattern. Stuff the wings, using a flower stick or similar to get the stuffing into the channels between the seams.

Fold the seam allowance inwards round the opening on the wings and sew the wings to the figure.

Make a curl in half of an approximately 10cm-long (4in) piece of zinc wire for the pig's tail and push the other half well into the pig.

Use a ready-made halo or make your own out of zinc wire and push the end of the wire into the pig's head.

If you like, you can tie a velvet ribbon round the pig's neck and attach two red berries for decoration.

A little dirt and glitter can be added to the pigs, as described in 'Effects' on page 12.

For details of making faces, see page 10.

ANGEL GEESE

YOU WILL NEED
White material
Thin fibre felt for the large goose
Material for feet
Stuffing
Terracotta-coloured craft paint
Halo
Velvet ribbon and red berries or similar
for decoration
The pattern is on page 141

A

INSTRUCTIONS

Note that the goose pattern is in two sizes, and that the larger one is divided up into two pieces to fit the page, but is assembled in the same way as the small one.

Read the information on 'Stuffed figures step by step' on page 11 before starting.

Cut a piece of material twice as large as the body. When sewing the large goose it is a good idea to reinforce the material by ironing an equally large sized piece of thin fibre felt onto the wrong side of the material. The fibre felt gives the large body a better shape.

Fold the material right side to right side and draw the outline of the body. Sew around, cut out, reverse, iron and stuff the body. Sew up the reversing opening.

Sew the wings and tack them onto the body as for the angel pig on page 46.

Fold material for the feet right side to right side

and draw two feet as in the pattern. Sew all the way around and cut out the feet. Cut a reversing opening through one layer of material as indicated in the pattern. Turn the feet inside out, stuff them and sew up the reversing opening.

If the goose is to be standing the two feet have to be tacked together first, as shown in Figure A. Then attach the feet under the body with pins so that the goose rests partly on its feet and partly on its rump. Adjust the position of the feet with pins until the goose balances properly and tack the feet in place. If you find this difficult, you could place the goose on a wreath as shown here.

Push a halo well into the head of the goose. If you like you can tie a velvet ribbon round the neck and with two red berries for decoration.

The geese have been brushed with a little ink from a stamp pad and a little glitter has been added as described on page 12. Paint the beak with terracotta-coloured craft paint and make a face as described on page 10.

Perhaps you have goose on your Christmas menu?

NEEDLEWORK SWEET CONES

YOU WILL NEED
Material for the cone

High-volume fibre felt

Material for the lining

Ribbon for hanging

The pattern is on page 135

INSTRUCTIONS
Iron the fibre felt onto the wrong side of a piece of material large enough for the whole pattern and then cut out an equally large piece of lining material.

Place the material with fibre felt and the lining material right side to right side and draw the pattern. First sew only the scalloped edge. Cut out the cone and cut slits in towards the seam between each of the scallops, as shown in Figure A.

Fold the material and lining away from each other and fold the whole cone inside out, right side to right side. Sew the open edges together. Leave a reversing opening in the lining, as shown in Figure B.

Cut off any surplus seam allowance and turn the cone inside out. Make sure you push the edges of the scallops completely out. Push the lining well down into the material part and iron the cone. Cut a piece of ribbon to allow you to hang the cone up and tack it in place on the inside of the cone.

Fill with sweets and hang up.

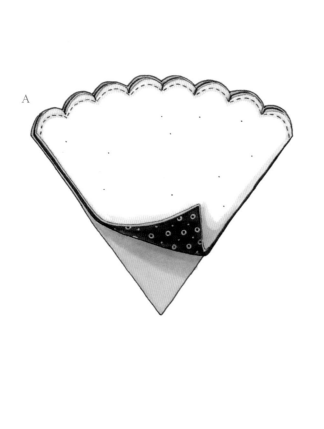
A

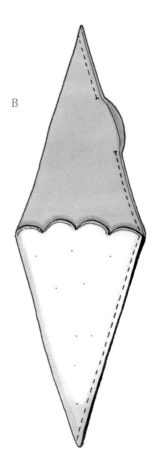
B

These little cloth cones with scalloped borders make lovely containers for sweets or pretty hanging decorations

MENUS AND PLACE CARDS

A

Make attractive place cards and matching menus to decorate your festive dining table. When your guests find out what they are going to be eating, their mouths will start to water…

The menus are made of fairly stiff scrapbook paper and decorated with suitable illustrations that are built out slightly on adhesive pads. If you like you can stiffen the pages by gluing them onto cardboard. A velvet ribbon is attached on the inside with double-sided tape for decoration.

The place cards are fashioned like small parcel labels with velvet ribbon that can be tied around the serviettes.

If you want to attach a loose menu, cut
out four slits inside the menu for the corners
using a sharp knife, or use photo corners, as
shown in Figure A. This means you can use
the menus several times

CAKE TABLE

A rich and romantic cake table with something for every taste is a very pleasant way to finish off a meal. Here we have small, delicious cheesecakes with redcurrants and strawberries, raspberry tarts, chocolate cake, cream cake, petits fours and a stunning traditional Norwegian almond ring cake.

You can decorate the table with holly leaves, but avoid using the berries; instead use redcurrants or imitation holly berries on wire. Just be sure to remove these before cutting the cake!

Small needlework muffins (as shown on pages 64–65), white crackers to delight the children, a string of Christmas lights and an angel in a chocolate-brown dress decorate the table.

APRON

YOU WILL NEED

Material for the apron and loop

Material for the apron strings

INSTRUCTIONS

Cut a strip of material measuring 15×80cm (6×31½in), adding a generous seam allowance along all the edges. Cut another strip measuring 30×80cm (12×31½in) with a wide seam allowance on one long edge and two short edges and about 4cm (1½in) of seam allowance on the final long edge. These 4cm (1½in) will make a wide fold at the bottom of the apron so that it hangs more neatly.

Sew the two strips together. Iron the generous seam allowances to each side and fold the frayed edge in towards the apron to hide it. Sew the two seam allowances together as shown in Figure A.

Fold the sides of the apron in twice, so that the frayed edge is hidden, and sew. Fold the bottom edge of the apron in twice in the same way, but here the fold should be 3cm (1¼in) wide; sew in place.

Cut out a piece of material measuring 5×10cm (2×4in) for a hanging loop and add a seam allowance. Fold in the seam allowance along the long edges and fold the loop double so that it is 2.5×10cm (1×4in).

Cut out a strip 230cm long and 7cm wide (90½×2¾in), adding a seam allowance. If you want you can sew together several shorter strips to make up a piece the right length. Fold the strip in the same way as the hanging loop, making it 3.5cm (1⅜in) wide, and iron it well. Also fold in and iron the ends of the strip.

Place the apron between the layers of the strip so that you have 90cm (35½in) on one side of the apron and 60cm (23½in) on the other side. Fold the hanging loop double and place it about 5cm (2in) from one side of the apron. Fix all the parts together using pins, as shown in Figure B.

Sew along the whole apron string so that the apron and hanging loop are fixed in place. Sew up the ends of the apron string. The apron string is tied on one side at the front, as shown in Figure C.

A

B

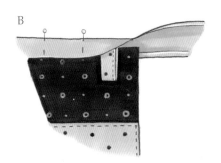

C

Sew an apron to match your outfit; it can be used for those times of the evening when you are constantly having to nip out to the kitchen to look after the cooking. A useful party apron...

THE KITCHEN

The kitchen is a hive of activity around Christmastime, and the
pixies are helping, of course. Pretty little cloth muffins,
coasters, tea towels and apples are some of the things
you'll find in the heart of the home.

The apron, here in red, is found on pages 56–57.

PIXIE GIRLS

YOU WILL NEED

Flesh-coloured fabric
Material for dress
Material for pantaloons
Material for apron
Stuffing
Craft paint for shoes
String for plaits and shoes
Figure stand if desired
The pattern is on page 136

A

B

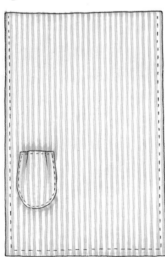

INSTRUCTIONS

The pixie girls are sewn the same way as the angels on pages 32–35, without the wings, but with the addition of aprons and hats.

APRON

Cut out a piece of material measuring 21×15cm (8¼×6in) and add a seam allowance. Fold inwards and sew the two long edges and one short edge.

Fold a piece of material large enough for the pocket right side to right side, draw the outline and sew all the way round the edge of the pocket. Cut out the pocket. Make a reversing opening through one of the material layers and turn the pocket inside out. Iron the pocket and fold two pleats, then sew along the edge of the pocket to fix the pleats, as shown in Figure A.

Place the pocket 5cm (2in) from the bottom edge of the apron and 1cm (⅜in) from the left-hand long edge. Sew the pocket in place as shown in Figure B. Tack the apron in place in folds over the skirt.

HAT

Fold a piece of woollen felt double, draw the outline of the hat as shown in the pattern and sew around it, as shown in Figure C. Cut out the hat. One of the edges (the back) at the opening of the hat should

correspond to the lowest dotted line in the pattern; the other (the front) is cut along the upper dotted curve. Cut along the line in the pattern.

Turn the hat inside out, as shown in Figure D. Make the hair as described on page 10. Pull the hat well down at the back and sides of the head and tack in place.

The shoes are painted on the feet using craft paint as described on page 10. The pixies' shoes are higher than the angels' and are painted up to the upper dotted line in the pattern. Make laces by tying a ribbon in a bow round the shoes.

PIXIE BOYS

YOU WILL NEED

Flesh-coloured fabric

Material for trousers

Woollen felt for coat

Woollen felt for hat

Stuffing

Paint for shoes

Cord for shoes

Materials to decorate coat

Doll stand if desired

The pattern is on pages 138–139

INSTRUCTIONS

Sew the body, arms and trousers as for the angel on pages 32–35.

COAT

Note that the pattern for the coat is marked with a fold line and should be cut double. The coat is sewn in two equal parts like a long sweater, with a collar. Fold a piece of woollen felt twice as large as the coat, draw the outline and sew all the way round the edge. Cut out the coat, noting that the openings are marked with dotted lines and should be cut along the line in the pattern. Cut the collar without a seam allowance.

You can decorate the coat with ribbon, glued or tacked on, and with small yo-yos. See the picture of the pixies, and the instructions for yo-yos on page 8.

Cut out the pocket as in the pattern and hand-sew it to the left-hand side of the coat about 4cm (1½in) from the bottom edge.

Put the coat on the pixie boy. Tack the collar around the neck as shown in Figure E and fold it down. Glue jewels on for buttons and if desired add a small sugar cane in the pocket. Make hair as described on page 10 and a hat as described on page 60. For details of making faces, see page 10.

C

D

E
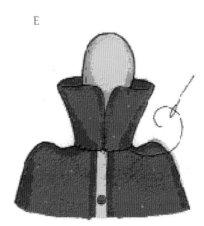

MUFFINS

YOU WILL NEED

Material for lower part and base

Thin fibre felt

Material for upper part

Plastic granules or similar

Stuffing

Red berries

The pattern is on page 142

INSTRUCTIONS

Note that the muffin pattern is in two sizes.

Iron the fibre felt onto the material for the lower part and base.

Place the material for the upper and lower parts right side to right side and sew along the curved edge as shown in Figure A. Cut out the part, remembering the seam allowance, and cut slits down to the seam between each scallop.

Cut out the small base, remembering the seam allowance. Because the bottom edge of the muffin part is curved, slits must be cut all the way round so that the base will fit, as shown in Figure B.

Sew on the base and sew up the open side as in Figure C.

Turn the muffin inside out, pushing all the curved seams well out. Push the upper part down into the lower part and iron the scallops. Sew a seam around the muffin as indicated by the dashed line in the pattern, as in Figure D.

Fold the upper part out again and stuff the muffin, begin by filling with plastic granules to make it stand right, and then follow with fibre stuffing. Fold in the seam allowance around the opening in the upper part, tack around the edge and gather to close up the muffin, as shown in Figure E. Decorate the top with two red berries.

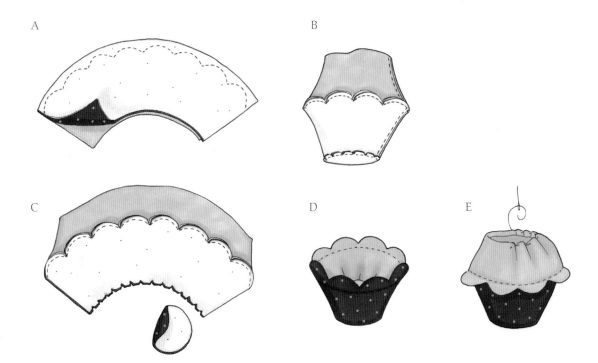

A

B

C

D

E

Pretty little muffins with cream make slightly untraditional but attractive decorations

MUFFIN APPLIQUÉS

YOU WILL NEED

Material for lower part
Material for upper part
Embroidery thread
Sand-coloured or brown stamp pad ink,
if desired
The pattern is on page 143

INSTRUCTIONS

Fold the material for the upper part right side to right side, trace the pattern and sew all the way round. Cut out and cut slits down to the seam between each scallop. Make a reversing opening through one of the material layers, turn the pocket completely inside out and iron.

Fold the material for the lower part right side to right side and sew around, leaving an opening at the top. Reverse through the opening. Sew both parts as shown in Figure A.

Tack the parts to the background so that the upper part conceals the opening in the lower part, as shown in Figure B.

Brush a little colour on the top edge of the scallops to make a shadow, as described in

'Effects' on page 12. Draw berries and holly leaves as shown in the pattern and embroider them with whole embroidery yarn as shown in Figure C.

Red jewels may also be added as berries.

A   B   C

MUFFIN TAPESTRY

YOU WILL NEED

Material for centre piece

Material for frame

Material for edges

High-volume fibre felt

Material for backing

Materials for muffins

Green embroidery thread

Jewels

INSTRUCTIONS

This is made the same way as the angel bust tapestry on pages 80–83, but is a different size.

Add seam allowances to all dimensions. The centre section of the tapestry measures 15×35cm (6×14in). Sew on strips of 35×3cm (14×1¼in) above and below the centre section. Then sew on strips of 21×3cm (8¼×1¼in) on each side. Iron on high-volume fibre felt and attach the back and edges as described on page 81. Sew on the muffins and embroider holly leaves as described on page 66. Quilt around the centre section and each muffin as described on page 81. Iron the piece before gluing on jewels, if desired.

COASTERS

YOU WILL NEED
Material for the coaster
High-volume fibre felt
Materials for muffins
Embroidery yarn for leaves and berries
The pattern is on page 143

INSTRUCTIONS
The size of the coasters can be varied, as long as they are large enough to fit the motif. The small coaster is 15cm (6in) in diameter and the large one 30cm (12in). Use a plate and a large cake-tray, for example, as templates.

Cut a piece of material twice as large as the desired size, adding a generous seam allowance. Find the centre of the material and draw the pattern for the needlework lettering using an invisible ink pen as described on page 10.

Sew backstitch with two threads of embroidery yarn to make the lettering.

Fold the pieces of material right side to right side and sew up the open side. Leave a reversing opening in the centre, as shown in Figure A.

Fold the part so that the seam is in the centre, add an equally large piece of high-volume fibre felt under, on the wrong side, and iron to attach it to the material. Draw the circle, making sure that the motif is in the centre, and sew around the edge. See Figure B.

Cut out the circle and turn it inside out. Sew and appliqué a muffin, as described on page 66, in the centre of the lettering. Embroider some leaves and berries to embellish the muffin.

Quilt around the lettering and muffin and around the edge of the large coaster, as described on page 67.

A
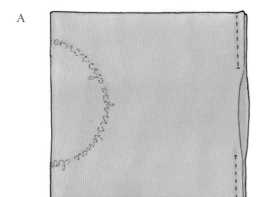

B
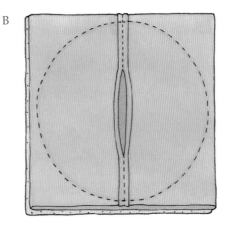

TEA TOWELS

Tea towels are easy to sew and make great Christmas presents. Use a rather coarse-woven material that is suitable for drying crockery and hands. You also need a drawstring hole.

Sew a small square to one corner before folding the edges of the towel inwards. Fold the edges in twice so that the frayed edge is hidden and sew. Finally, press on a drawstring hole in the reinforced square for hanging the towel.

HEARTS

Sew hearts in woollen felt or other material and decorate with yo-yos, buttons, felt dots and jewels as described on page 8.

Hearts can be found in four sizes in the pattern on page 152. Read the section on 'Stuffed figures step by step' on page 11 for advice before starting the project.

A garland of apples…

APPLES

YOU WILL NEED

Material for the apple

Embroidery yarn

Pointed wooden stick

Dark brown craft paint

Stuffing

The pattern is on page 142

INSTRUCTIONS

Fold material for the apple right side to right side and draw on the outline. Sew around the apple and add an extra seam allowance at the opening as indicated by 'ES' in the pattern (see Figure A).

Cut out, turn inside out and iron the apple. Fold the seam allowance in and iron.

Sew around the opening with embroidery yarn using a long needle or bodkin. Stuff the apple so it stands up nice and firmly and then gather the opening. Sew right through the apple and back

again, as shown in Figure B. Tighten the yarn to make a hollow on the top and bottom sides of the apple.

Cut about 5cm (2in) off the wooden stick and pointen one end using a pencil sharpener if necessary. Paint the stick dark brown, let it dry and twist the stick through the material, well into the apple so that about 2cm (¾in) protrudes, as shown in the illustration.

A

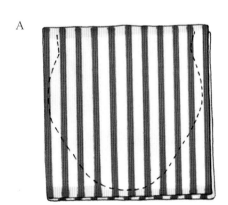

B

ADULT BEDROOM

In the bedroom, angel busts create a peaceful, cosy atmosphere. Blanket ponchos and double-thick woollen felt slippers help you keep warm on cold winter evenings. Here you will also find beautiful presents for girlfriends, make-up bags, rings and pins.

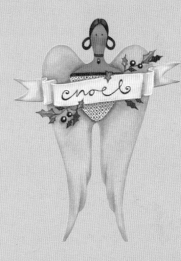

ANGEL BUSTS

YOU WILL NEED

Flesh-coloured fabric
Material for dress
Material for wings
Stuffing
Thin fibre felt if necessary
Ribbon and jewels for necklace
Halo
Doll stand if desired
The pattern is on page 143

A

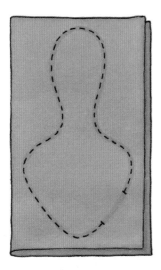

B

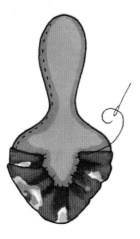

INSTRUCTIONS

The wings here are slightly different from the wings for the angels on pages 32–35, but the procedure for sewing them is exactly the same.

Fold material for the bust right side to right side and draw the outline of the bust as in the pattern. Sew around the outline, as shown in Figure A, remembering the seam allowance.

Stuff the bust and sew up the reversing opening. Cut out a piece of material about 10×7cm (4×2¾in). Fold two small pleats on each side and attach with pins to the back of the bust. Fold the rest of the material around and tack in place on the back, as shown in Figure B.

Make the hair and face as described on page 10. Use a ready-made halo or make one out of zinc wire and push it well into the angel's head. Attach a narrow ribbon and a jewel as a necklace around the neck. Tack the bust firmly to the wings. Cut the rod of a doll stand to the desired length, sharpen the tip and twist the rod into the wings and some distance into the body so that the angel is held steady.

77

ANGEL BUST APPLIQUÉS

YOU WILL NEED

Flesh-coloured fabric

Material for dress

Material for wings

Brown craft paint

Sand-coloured or brown stamp pad ink, if desired

A little stuffing

Embroidery thread

Cord and jewels for decoration

The pattern is on page 144

INSTRUCTIONS

Fold material for the wings, body and dress right side to right side. Trace the parts and sew around the edges, as in Figure A. Cut out the parts and cut slits into the seam allowance where the edge curves inwards; turn the parts inside out and iron. The dress is turned inside out through an opening made in one of the layers of material.

Paint hair on the head using dark brown craft paint or textile paint. Push a little stuffing into the body and tie a cord around the neck to form the angel's necklace.

If you like, you can brush the angel's wings with a little stamp pad ink as described on page 12 to create a shadow effect.

Place the wings, bust and dress on the background material and attach using pins. The dress should have a pleat at the top, as shown in Figure B. Adjust the positioning until you are satisfied and then tack the parts into place.

Sew decorative seams with brown thread on the wings as indicated by the dotted line in the pattern. Sew the plaits on each side of the head using brown embroidery thread, and attach the halo using brown thread. Make a face as described on page 10 and glue on jewels for decoration. Although the jewels are attached firmly using jewellery adhesive, the angel here should not be washed in a washing machine.

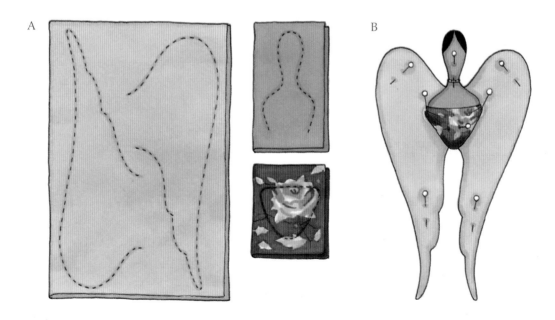

A   B

Sew an angel bust onto a cushion...

ANGEL BUST TAPESTRY

YOU WILL NEED
Material for centre piece
Materials for framework
Material for edging
Material for yo-yos
Buttons
Jewels
Embroidery thread
*Materials for angel bust as
described on page 77*
The pattern is on page 144.

INSTRUCTIONS
Add seam allowances to all
dimensions. The centre section
measures 15×38cm (6×15in).
Sew a strip of 38×4cm (15×1½in)
on each long edge. Sew a strip of
23×4cm (9×1½in) on each short
edge, see Figure A.

Sew the parts of the angel bust,
described on page 77 and fix
with pins to make it easier to
position the lettering and halo.
Transfer the lettering pattern
and the halo as described on
page 10, and remove the angel.
Stitch the lettering using
backstitch, using two strands of
embroidery thread. Sew on the
halo using brown thread.

Iron high-volume fibre felt
onto the wrong side of the
tapestry and place a backing
piece as large as the blanket
behind the fibre felt. Sew a
zigzag seam around the edge to
keep the layers together.

EDGING
Cut 3cm-wide (1¼in) strips
and join them together so that
they go all the way around the
tapestry. Start in one corner,
placing the material strip right
side to right side against the
motif side of the tapestry. Sew
on the strip about 6mm (¼in)
from the edge, as shown in
Figure B.

When you get to a corner, stop
your seam about 6mm (¼in)
from the edge, as shown in

Figure C. Fold the strip as
shown in Figure D before
continuing sewing.

When the strip has been sewn
in place round the entire
tapestry, fold it in round the
edge and tack it in place, as
shown in Figure F.

QUILTING
Quilt around the centre
section of the tapestry and
around the angel.

When quilting, sew through all the layers so that the stitches are also visible on the reverse side. The stitches are short – about 1mm (¹⁄₁₆in) – on the front, and about 5–7mm (¼in) on the back. Pull the thread tight as you go so that the stitches make small hollows in the material. Sew yo-yos as described on page 8 from circles of about 6 and 10cm (2⅜ and 4in) plus seam allowance. Iron the tapestry carefully with a cloth over it before attaching yo-yos, buttons and jewels.

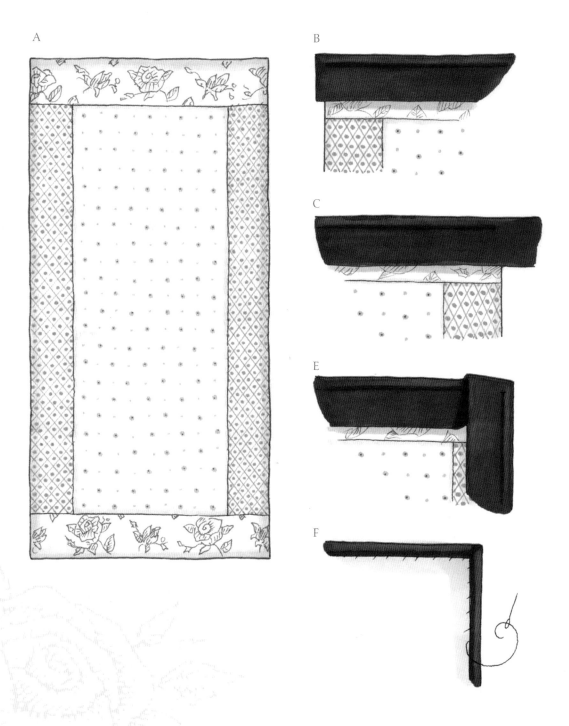

wish you
a

BLANKET PONCHO

YOU WILL NEED
Woollen felt
Material for edges
Materials for decoration

INSTRUCTIONS
Cut two 80×80cm (31½×31½in) squares of woollen felt, add a seam allowance and place the parts right side to right side.

Draw a 22×22cm (8¾×8¾in) square in one corner to make it easier to draw the neck and shoulders. Following the lines of the square, measure and mark 5cm (2in) in from the edge. Draw a gentle curve between these points. On the other side of each of the points, draw a gentle curve the other way, so that the shoulders are rounded off, as in Figure A.

Sew a cosy blanket poncho
to keep you warm on frosty
winter days. The poncho
is extra-large with a wide
neck – like a cross between
a blanket and a poncho

Sew from the curve and down along each side of the poncho. Cut away the material outside the curve and cut the neck opening as in Figure B.

Cut 7.5cm-wide (3in) strips (which includes the seam allowance) and join them together to make two strips, each long enough to edge half of the poncho's bottom edge. Start at one tip of the poncho, placing the strip right side to right side about 2.5cm (1in) in from the corner. Sew the strip along one edge, as in Figure C. The seam will then be about 3cm (1¼in) in from the edge.

When you reach the other tip of the poncho, stop sewing 2.5cm (1in) from the corner and cut off surplus edge material. Fold the strip in and around the edge and tack it onto the backing piece. Sew the next strip about 2.5cm (1in) from the edge, but the tip of the strip should extend beyond the edge of the poncho and the seam should go all the way to the edge as shown in Figure D. Finish the other tip the same way. Fold the seam allowance round the tip before folding the rest of the strip in and around the edge. Tack in place. Edge the neck in the same way, using one strip all the way round.

The children's size poncho is 60×60cm (23½×23½in) plus seam allowance. Use a 17×17cm (6¾×6¾in) square and measure 4cm (1½in) in from the edge to draw the neck. The edges are of the same width as those on the adult's size poncho.

Decorate the poncho with yo-yos, as described on page 8, or with the pretty bird motifs as shown on page 37.

A

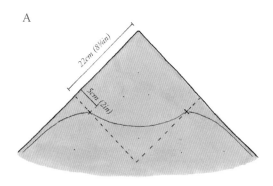

B

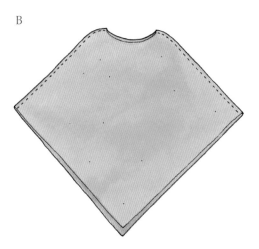

C

D

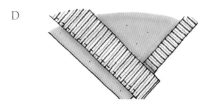

Sew a child's blanket poncho with bird motif

SLIPPERS

YOU WILL NEED
Woollen felt

Materials for decoration

The pattern is on page 145

INSTRUCTIONS
The pattern is in two sizes: the small one is a children's size 5 to 8½, and the large one is a ladies' size 3 to 7. If you need another size enlarge or reduce the pattern using a photocopier.

The slipper is of double thickness and has a fold line as indicated in the pattern; there is no difference between the left and right foot.

Cut out two complete slipper parts for one slipper and place them right side to right side. Sew from point A to point B on the upper and lower side of the slipper part as indicated in the pattern. See Figure B.

Now fold the double slipper part the other way, so that the seams lie parallel to each other in the centre of the slipper.

Decide which part is to be the lining and fix a pin in it to remind you. Allow the seams to lie slightly inside the edge of this part when you continue, approximately as indicated by the dotted line in the pattern. It is a good idea to make this part slightly smaller, as it will then fit better inside the slipper and not curl up so easily.

Now sew the instep and heel closed and leave a reversing opening in the heel seam on the lining part, as shown in Figure B.

Sew up the opening at the back and front as shown in Figure C.

Cut off any surplus seam allowance and turn the slipper inside out. Fit the lining part into the outer part, pushing it well into the slipper.

Lay a wet tea towel over the slipper and iron it well so that the felt is compressed and seems thinner.

Decorate the slipper with circle ornaments, as described on page 8, or make holes through both layers around the opening and thread a ribbon through, finishing off with a bow at the front.

A
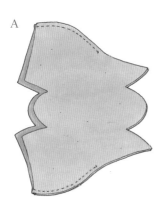

B
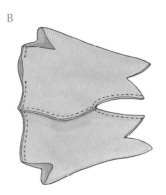

C
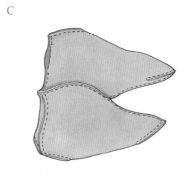

Cosy, warm winter slippers

PURSES

Make useful and pretty presents for your girlfriends

YOU WILL NEED
Material
Material for lining
High-volume fibre felt
Button or press stud
The pattern is on page 145

INSTRUCTIONS
The pattern is provided in two sizes: the smaller makes a useful coin purse while the larger is ideal as a make-up bag.

Cut the whole purse shape out of material, lining material and high-volume fibre felt.

Cut out the part without the flap, up to the dotted line in the pattern, in material, lining

material and fibre felt. Remember to add a generous seam allowance.

Iron the pieces of high-volume fibre felt onto the wrong side of the pieces of material and then place the corresponding pieces of material and lining material right side to right side. Sew up the curved edge of the flap of the purse and then sew up the top of the part without the flap, as shown in Figure A.

Fold the material and lining apart and place the two parts right side to right side so that material is lying against material and lining lies against lining.

Sew around the edge as shown in Figure B, leaving a reversing opening at the bottom of the lining part.

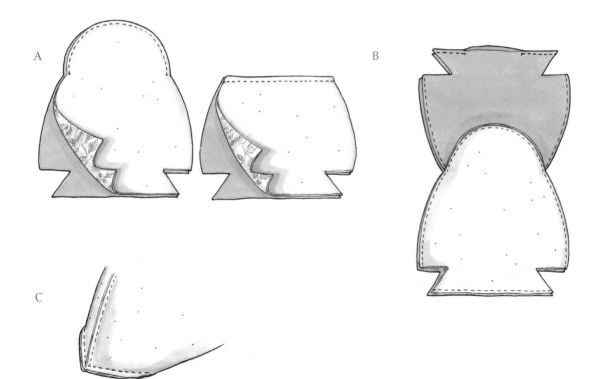

A

B

C

Now fold the corners so that the seams at the edges and base are parallel to each other and sew the corners closed. See Figure C.

Cut away surplus seam allowance, turn inside out and iron the purse.

Fasten a press stud top piece through the flap and a bottom piece through the front of the purse to close it. You can also use a button and button hole.

RINGS AND PINS

Yo-yos can be used to make lovely rings and pins. Rings and pins with holes for attachment are available in craft shops. Small yo-yos, as described on page 8, can be used to decorate rings

CARD TREE

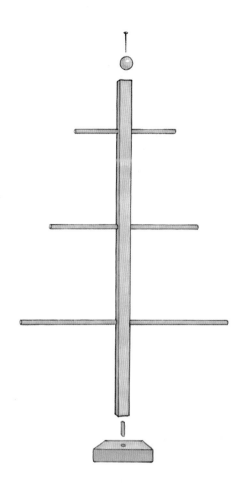

YOU WILL NEED

Base, approx. 10×10×2.5cm (4×4×1in)

Centre rod, approx. 2×2×55cm (¾×¾×21½in)

Large flower sticks, 6mm (¼in) in diameter

Wooden ball, 2.5cm (1in) in diameter

Nails

Wood glue

White paint

Drill (6mm/¼in)

Hammer

INSTRUCTIONS

Wooden boards and laths to make the base and the central rod can be bought at lumber yards.

Drill a 6mm (¼in) hole in the centre of the base and a hole in the middle of the bottom end of the centre rod, and use a piece of a flower stick and some wood glue to attach the rod to the base.

Measure 15cm (6in) up from the bottom of the rod and drill a hole, then drill the next two holes 15cm (6in) apart. This will leave about 9cm (3½in) to the top of the rod.

Cut three flower sticks, 35, 25 and 17cm long (13¾, 10, 6¾in). Push these through the holes in the central rod and glue them in place if necessary. Fix the stick tree to the base

and attach the ball to the top with a nail as shown in the illustration. Paint the tree in the desired colour. White-painted 5cm-long (2in) clothes pegs can be used to attach the Christmas cards.

You can make a larger stick tree to stand on the floor by enlarging all the dimensions.

Display your Christmas cards on a tree stand

GIRL'S BEDROOM

This girl is a little angel with checked wings and her own four-poster bed. In her bedroom she has a Christmas tree, decorated with little dresses and sweaters. There are Christmas stockings and a neat advent calendar with pouches full of presents — waiting for Christmas isn't easy.

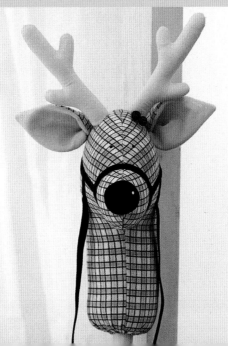

BABUSHKA DOLLS

YOU WILL NEED

Material for headscarf and body

Material for face

Stuffing

Appliqué paper

Paint for the hair

Plastic granules or similar

Ribbon and jewels for decoration if desired

The pattern is on page 151

INSTRUCTIONS

The pattern is in three sizes, the smallest of which is suitable for hanging on a Christmas tree. If you want the babushka doll to stand, it is a good idea to use plastic granules or some similar material to add weight at the base.

Sew together a piece of material for the headscarf and a piece of material for the body. Fold the joined pieces right side to right side and draw the outline of the doll so that the join between the two materials lies approximately at the dotted line in the pattern.

Note that the corners that are turned in to form the base shall be open, in addition to the reversing opening, and sew around the outline as shown in Figure A.

Cut out the figure and fold and sew the bottom corners so that the seams are parallel to each other and form a base, as shown in Figure B.

Turn inside out, iron and stuff the doll. Babushka dolls that are to stand should be stuffed with padding first and then with plastic granules in the base.

If you want to tie a ribbon around the doll, it should be cut to fit the slanting shape of the doll. You can do this by folding the ends of the ribbon right side to right side, in towards the centre. Make sure that the ribbon is long enough for the ends to overlap each other and is twice the width of the figure. Sew a seam across the ribbon, inside the fold on each side, parallel to the sides of the doll, as in Figure C. Turn the ribbon so that the right side is outwards and fix it around the figure.

Iron appliqué paper onto a small piece of material to make the face and peel off the backing paper. Cut out the face and paint hair as shown in the pattern, as described in 'Painting details' on page 10. Iron the face onto the figure and make eyes and rosy cheeks as described on page 10.

A

B

C

Babushkas in many colours

CHRISTMAS STOCKINGS

LINED STOCKING

Cut a piece of material and a piece of lining material twice as large as the stocking, and sew these pieces together. Fold the parts right side to right side, draw the outline of a stocking against the fold line on each side of the seam and sew around. Leave a reversing opening in the lining, as shown in figure A.

Cut out the stocking and turn it inside out. Then push the lining part down into the stocking and iron.

A

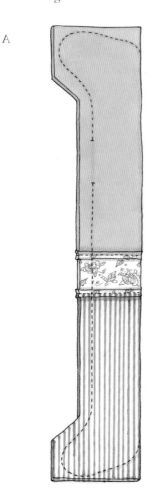

SIMPLE STOCKING

Stiffen the material with fibre felt if desired before you start.

Fold the material for the stocking double, right side to right side, draw the stocking outline against the fold line and sew around the edge. Make a generous seam allowance at the top of the stocking.

Cut out, turn inside out and iron the stocking. Fold the edge in twice so that the frayed edge is hidden and sew around the opening to finish off.

On the woollen felt stocking you only need to fold the edge in once and tack the edge to the inside without stitching through the felt.

Sew on a loop or use ribbon for hanging. Decorate the stocking with yo-yos if desired as described on page 8.

The pattern is on page 146.

POUCH ADVENT CALENDAR

YOU WILL NEED

Material for front and pouches

Material for backing

High-volume fibre felt

10.5mm (³⁄₈in) drawstring holes

Two wooden laths, about 70×2cm (27½×1in)

INSTRUCTIONS

Cut material for the front, high-volume fibre felt and material for the back, measuring 103×72cm (40½×28¼in), adding seam allowances. Iron the high-volume fibre felt to the wrong side of the material for the front.

Cut four 72×16cm (28¼×6¼in) strips of material for the pouches, adding a seam allowance, and add an extra-wide seam allowance on the upper long edge.

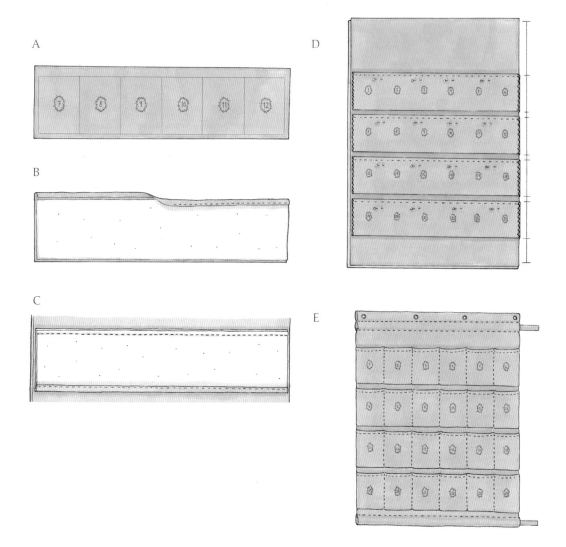

A

B

C

D

E

Cut four 72×16cm (28¼×6¼in) strips of fibre felt, with seam allowances only along the two short edges and one of the long edges.

The calendar dates are stamped on using a ready-made calendar date stamp set and a textile ink pad.

Measure the pouches and draw the outlines with an invisible ink pen on the right side of each strip. Each pouch should measure 12×16cm (4¾×6¼in). Stamp the numbers on the material as described on page 9. First attach the wreath about 6.5cm (2½in) from the bottom of the pocket, followed by the number in the centre of the wreath, as shown in Figure A. Alternatively, you could embroider the dates on the calendar.

Iron high-volume fibre felt onto the wrong side of the strips of pouches so that the edges of the material and fibre felt correspond along the bottom and each short edge. There should be a seam allowance in the material only along the top long edge.

Fold the seam allowance at the top in twice so that the frayed edge is hidden and sew, as in Figure B.

The bottom of the pouch strip is fastened to the front of the calendar, hanging down with the wrong side outwards, as shown in Figure C, and is then folded upwards. Attach the top of the pouch strip with pins and sew a zigzag seam along each side.

Attach the bottom pouch strip 10cm (4in) from the bottom edge of the calendar, fold it upwards and attach the next strip 2cm (1in) above it, and so on, as shown in Figure D. At the end, there should be about 23cm (9in) left at the top of the calendar.

Place the back of the calendar right side to right side on the front and sew along the two long edges. Turn the calendar inside out and fix the layers together with zigzag seams at the top and bottom.

Sew seams 12cm (4¾in) apart across the pouch strips to make six pouches in each row. Make sure the layers are correctly positioned relative to each other by ironing and use pins or stitches that can be removed later.

Fold the seam allowance at the top inwards towards the back of the calendar, followed by 8.5cm (3⅜in) of the material at the top. Sew a seam 8cm (3¼in) from the top to attach the fold.

Then sew a seam 4cm (1¾in) down from the top of the calendar to divide the 8cm-wide (3¼in) area into two 4cm-wide (1¾in) areas. Fold the bottom 4.5cm (1¾in) of the calendar in towards the back and sew in the same way.

Press on four drawstring holes at the top for hanging, as described on the packet. Cut out two 70cm (27½in) lengths of wooden lath and thread one into the 4cm (1¾in) channel under the drawstring holes and one at the bottom, as shown in Figure E.

ANGEL WINGS

YOU WILL NEED
Material for wings and ribbon
Fibre felt
Stuffing
The pattern is on pages 148–149

INSTRUCTIONS
Cut a 150×4.5cm (59×1¾in) strip (or, if necessary, join together shorter strips to make up the length), and cut two more strips measuring 7×4.5cm (2¾×1¾in). These measurements include seam allowances.

Fold the seam allowance on each long edge inwards and fold the strips double to make one strip about 150×1.5cm (59×⅝in) and two 7×1.5cm (2¾×⅝in). Sew along the open edges and sew in the seam allowance at each end of the long strips.

Sew wings as in the wing pattern for the large angel, as described on page 130. Fold the short strips double and put them in place through the reversing opening at the bottom of the wings before tacking the opening closed.

Attach the centre of the long strip at the top centre of the wings and thread the ends of the strip through the loops on the underside of the wings as in the illustration.

Tie a bow on the back so that the strips sit firmly on the shoulders.

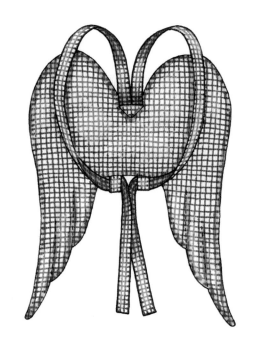

A little angel...
Well, sometimes, maybe

MINIATURE GARMENTS

When sewing material to make small garments, you should first iron on stiffening fibre felt, which holds the material together and prevents the edges fraying. Woollen felt does not fray.

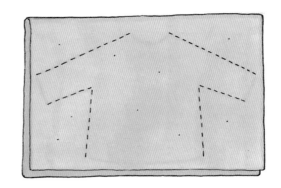

Fold a piece of material with fibre felt or a piece of felt right side to right side and trace the pattern. Sew around the outlines, as shown in Figure A, and cut out. Cut along the lines without a seam allowance. Turn inside out and decorate with ribbon or embroidery yarn and jewels.

These small coat hangers were bought ready-made, but you can also make your own from zinc wire or similar.

The pattern is on page 147.

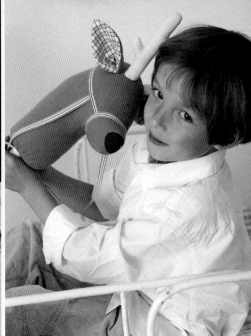

BOY'S BEDROOM

This boy really loves his hobby reindeer, but a lot of teddy bears live here too. His room is decorated with a long garland of flags made of paper triangles folded over and glued onto string. Small presents are packed in scrapbook paper with monster and car motifs, and there is a ladder for hanging up advent calendar stockings.

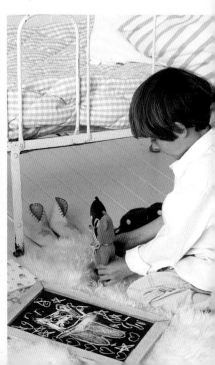

SIMPLE TEDDY BEARS

YOU WILL NEED
Material
Paint for the snout
Ribbon for bow
Stuffing
The pattern is on page 147

INSTRUCTIONS
The pattern comes in two sizes; the small teddy bears can be used for decorations or on the tree, and the large ones are suitable for use as toys.

Fold the material double, right side to right side, and draw the outline of a body and two ears. Note that there should be openings for the ears in addition to the reversing opening. Sew around the body and ears and cut out. Turn the ears inside out and position Them in the openings for the ears in the body; sew in place as shown in Figure A.

Turn the body inside out, iron it and stuff it before sewing up the reversing opening. Tie two strands of embroidery yarn or similar tightly round the neck, as far down towards the arms as possible, so as to form a clear break between the head and the body. Paint the snout as described on page 10. If you want a rustic effect you can brush the teddy with a little textile stamp pad ink using a dry paintbrush, as described on page 12. Sew a stitch using sewing thread of a suitable colour down from the snout and two stitches in each foot to make claws, as in Figure B. Tie a bow around the neck.

The haloes on the small teddy bears are attached in the same way as for the angels on pages 32–35.

A
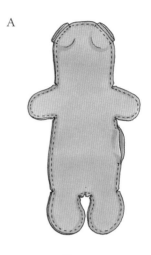

B

DRUMS

YOU WILL NEED

Material for top and bottom, sides and edges

Stiffening fibre felt

Stuffing

Brown velvet ribbon or similar

Stiff cardboard

Embroidery yarn

Cord for hanging, if desired

The patterns for circles on drums are on page 134

INSTRUCTIONS

The pattern comes in two sizes. The large drum is sewn from a strip of material 41×10cm (16×4in) and two strips 41×3.5cm (16×1⅜in). The small drum is sewn from a strip of material 16.5×4cm (6½×1¾in) and two strips 16.5×1.5cm (6½×⅝in). Add seam allowances to all parts.

Sew the narrow strips to the wide strip as shown in Figure A. Iron the seam allowances between the strips away from each other and iron stiffening fibre felt onto the wrong side of the drum piece. Also iron stiffening fibre felt onto the wrong side of a piece of material large enough to make the circles. Draw the outline of two circles as in the pattern, with a seam allowance, and cut out. Sew a circle onto each end of the drum piece. The reversing opening on the side of the drum must be as long as the diameter of the circle, as shown in Figure B. Turn the drum inside out.

Cut out two circles (without seam allowances) from stiff cardboard. Push the circles in through the reversing opening so that they are located at the top and base of the drum. Stuff the drum and sew up the reversing opening.

Sew a large zigzag seam up and down the sides of the drum with embroidery yarn. Attach a cord for hanging on each side of the drum at the join between the edge and centre part, and attach brown velvet ribbon or similar round the upper edge to hide the attachments of the cord, as shown in Figure C. On the small drum the velvet ribbon is folded double to make in narrower. The large drum has a velvet ribbon for hanging instead of cord, and a small star is sewn on the top.

For an antique appearance you can brush the drum with textile stamp pad ink, as described on page 12.

A

B C

115

HOBBY REINDEER

YOU WILL NEED

Material for reindeer
Material for antlers
Lining material for ears
Stuffing
Ribbon for bridle
Paint for snout
Red berries for decoration if
desired
Wooden dowel about 2–2.5cm
(1in) diameter and 1m
(39½in) long, available from
lumber yards
Paint for dowel
The pattern is on page 150

INSTRUCTIONS

Fold the material for the head
right side to right side and
draw the outline of the head;
fold the material for the antlers
right side to right side and
draw the outline of the antlers.

A

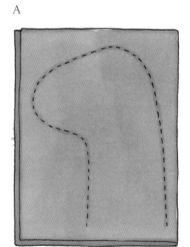

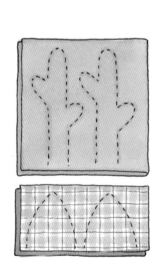

B

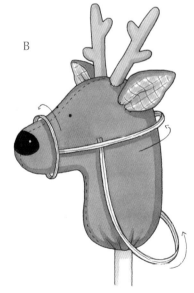

116

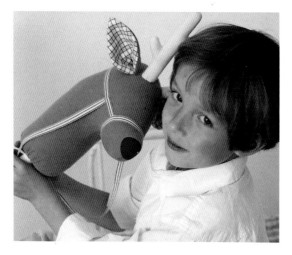

Place the material for the ears and the lining material right side to right side and draw the ears. Sew around the parts, as shown in Figure A. Cut out, turn the parts inside out and iron as described on page 11. Stuff the head and antlers firmly.

Paint the wooden dowel in the desired colour.

Fold the seam allowance round the opening at the neck inwards and tack around it. Twist the dowel a little way up into the neck and gather the material around it; fix firmly in place by sewing several times around.

Fold the seam allowance at the opening inwards and fold the ears double; attach the head with pins. Fold in the seam allowance at the base of the antlers and attach the antlers with pins. Adjust the antlers and ears until you are satisfied with their positions and tack in place. Paint the snout as described on page 10.

Cut a piece of ribbon to go from the muzzle, round the back of the head and back to the muzzle, as well as a piece to go round the muzzle. Cut about 60cm (23½in) of ribbon for the reins and attach the ribbons as in Figure B.

The reindeer on the wall is sewn in the same way, but the neck is about 7cm (2¾in) shorter, as indicated by the thin dotted line in the pattern.

STOCKING ADVENT CALENDAR

Small Christmas stockings can be used to make an appealing advent calendar; if you don't want to make all 24 stockings, you could take a shortcut and use a mixture of stockings and parcels, as shown here.

Use the larger of the small Christmas stocking patterns and the largest star, as described on page 146. For instructions for making the Christmas stocking, see the project on page 101.

STARS
The dates are stamped on as described on page 9 before the stars are sewn on.

Fold the material right side to right side, sew round the edge and cut out. Make a reversing opening through one of the material layers, turn inside out and iron.

The pattern is on page 146.

CHRISTMAS WORKSHOP

The workshop is full of hustle and bustle before Christmas. Here you will find cloth giftbags filled with presents for friends and family and packages wrapped in pretty paper, tied up with colourful ribbon. But can everyone wait for their presents until Christmas?

CLOTH GIFT BAGS

YOU WILL NEED
Material

Stiffening fibre felt

INSTRUCTIONS

The instructions do not contain any dimensions as the bag can be sewn in any size to suit the gifts you are giving.

Iron stiffening fibre felt onto a piece of material as wide as the desired size of the bag and as long as twice the bag's height plus the base. Fold the material and fibre felt right side to right side. Sew up one open side and turn inside out. Fold half of the bag into itself so that it becomes half as high and twice as stiff. Sew a seam across at the bottom, holding all the layers together, as shown in Figure A. Now sew across the corners and cut them off on the outside of the seam, as in Figure B. The base gets wider the further you sew from the corners. Turn the bag inside out. Sew the handles as described on page 19. Sew a seam around the edge of the opening, attaching the handles at the same time.

A

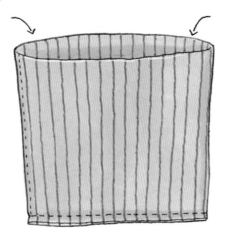

B

CARDS AND PACKAGING

Wrapping up presents and making cards is a true pleasure because of the wide variety of paper, paper decorations and ribbons available today. Often, you don't need to do anything very advanced to create impact. Scrapbook paper may be used as wrapping paper for smaller presents.

Many households now have a digital camera and printer, so cards can be made from photographs in no time. Print out on matt photo paper, cut out and attach a drawstring hole at one corner for the ribbon.

Yo-yos make pretty decorations for particularly special presents. Follow the instructions set out on page 8.

GIFT IDEAS

GIFT BOX WITH CARD AND ENVELOPE

Make a number of similar cards and decorate a box with the same motif. Put the cards and envelopes in the box, and you have a fine set of cards to give away. Here I have used a cardboard box of a suitable size and painted it white before covering it with paper. Create an antique effect for the box and cards in the same way as for cut-out pictures on pages 40–41.

A SWEET PRESENT FOR A CHILD

A pair of small slippers, some sweets and a little teddy bear make a lovely present for a child.

A PRESENT FOR A GIRLFRIEND

The muffins on pages 64–65 make excellent pin cushions. Add a piece of material and a small pair of pink scissors in a needlework gift bag and you have a great gift for a girlfriend.

A PRESENT FROM THE KITCHEN

Stamp a border on material as described on page 9 and sew it into small spice bags. Fill with spices or similar and write the contents on the border with an indelible pen. Decorate the lid of a couple of jars of jelly or jam. For example, you can use wrapping paper, ribbon and berries. Put everything into a checked gift bag.

I have decorated this outdoor space with lanterns, fir trees and wreaths – and a beautiful large angel propped up in a metal bucket. Remember to leave out some food for the birds

LARGE ANGEL

The angel is made in the same way as the ones on pages 32–35, but this one is 80cm (31½in) tall. The pattern is on pages 148–149. In order to stand firmly, the angel needs the support of a solid pole, which can be bought from a lumber yard. Standing in a bucket of earth, covered with moss or spruce twigs, the angel stands 110cm (43¼in) high and is a proper 'welcome' angel.

ACKNOWLEDGMENTS

THE PEOPLE (AND ONE DOG)

Photographer Grethe Syvertsen Arnstad and Ingrid Skonfar: thank you again for enjoyable and creative days doing the photography. You are wonderful, and this book would not have been possible without your fantastic efforts.

Also a big thank you to my publisher Karin Mundal and Cappelen forlag.

Unni Dahl deserves a big thank you for her graphic design for the book.

Eirin – Many thanks for your help, and all the best for the future.
Torje – The best husband in the world – many thanks yet again.
Totto – the best dog in the world and a constant companion.
Jørn and Tove, thank you for your help.

The models Synne and Luis were wonderful, and I would also like to thank your mothers, Nina and Sunniva.

The cakes were specially made by Marion at Konditori Elliott.

The baker who made the Norwegian almond ring cake, also deserves a big thank you.

INTERIOR DECORATION

I would like to thank the following shops, local to me. I bought most of the beautiful props you see in the book in these places. They are all run by very helpful, able ladies.
PS: Some of the props are private, but I do most of my shopping in these places:

TINNIES HUS – A beautiful interior decorating shop with a good selection of furniture and all sorts of accessories. The owners travel a lot to obtain their goods, ensuring that the shop's selection is exciting and inspiring. I never go to Tønsberg without visiting them.

LANDROMANTIKK – A gloriously whimsical, shabby secondhand shop, mainly for online shopping, but open for visiting on certain days. The owner is a really charming lady with a taste for rural romanticism.

MILDE HIMMEL – A little bit of candy in the centre of Sandefjord with lots of wonderful gifts, cushions, blankets and other things you just have to own.

FRISK BRIS – A cheerful shop with branches in Borgheim and Hvasser. Something for all tastes, whether you like maritime themes or rich romanticism.

TORNEROSE – This is a beautiful, richly stocked and tasteful florist's shop. Like going into a French courtyard, but in Tønsberg.

The beautiful sheepskins were supplied by www.ferderfaar.no

SUPPLIERS

Coast and Country Crafts & Quilts
Tel: 01872 863894
www.coastandcountrycrafts.co.uk

Coats and Clark USA
PO Box 12229
Greenville SC29612-0229
Tel: 0800 648 1479
www.coatsandclark.com

Connecting Threads
13118 NE 4th Street
Vancouver
WA 9884
email: customerservice@connecting threads.com
www.customerservice @connectingthreads.com

Creative Quilting
32 Bridge Road
East Molesey
KT8 9HA
Tel: 020 941 7075
email: info@creativequilting.co.uk
www.creativequilting.co.uk

eQuilter.com
5455 Spine Road, Suite E
Boulder
CO 80301
email: service@equilter.com
www.eQuilter.com

Fred Aldous Ltd.
37 Lever Street
Manchester
Tel: 08707 517301
www.fredaldous.co.uk

Panduro Hobby
Westway House
Transport Avenue
Brentford
Tel: 020 8566 1680
www.panduro.co.uk

Quiltzauberei.de
Marschallstr. 9
46539 Dinslaken
Germany
Tel: +49 2064 827980
www.quiltzauberei.de

The Fat Quarters
5 Choprell Road
Blackhall Mill
Newcastle
Tel: 01207 565728
www.thefatquarters.co.uk

The Sewing Bee
52 Hillfoot Street
Dunoon
Argyll
Tel: 01369 706879
www.thesewingbee.co.uk

Threads and Patches
48 Aylesbury Street
Fenny Stratford, Bletchley
Tel: 01908 649687
www.threadsandpatches.co.uk

PATTERNS

A page reference for the pattern can be found in the instructions for each project.

Important: A seam allowance must be made on each part of the pattern, except for the areas that are marked with a dotted line (see below).

Areas that are marked with a dashed line indicate a normal-to-wide seam allowance, except where the line represents a dividing line in the pattern.

THE APPLIQUÉS will appear somewhat smaller when the sewing is completed. If you prefer to make appliqués using appliqué paper, cut it 1–2mm (⅛in) inside the pattern edges for the best result.

KEY TO SYMBOLS
WSA: Wrong Side Appliqués. Appliqués in which the figure is sewn from two layers of material in the same way as a stuffed figure, before being fixed to the background.

ES: Extra Seam Allowance. This is indicated where it is particularly important.

It is folded inwards along the inner dotted line, except where it is to fit inside another part such as a leg of an angel or pixie.

Always sew out seam allowances that end at an opening.

DOTTED LINE indicates an opening or the join between two pieces of material.

DASHED LINE indicates a non-fraying edge of woollen felt that ca be simply cut off.

FOLD LINES mean that the pattern should be mirror-imaged on the other side of the line.

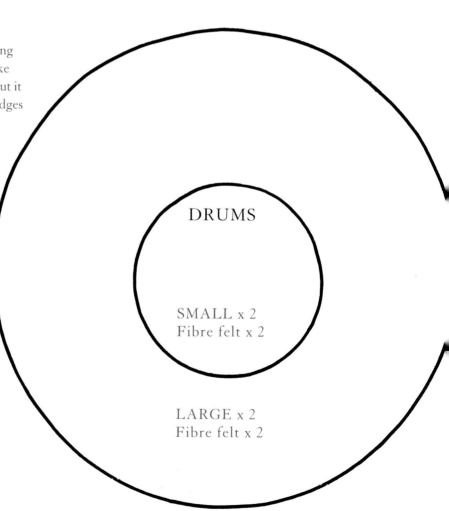

DRUMS

SMALL x 2
Fibre felt x 2

LARGE x 2
Fibre felt x 2

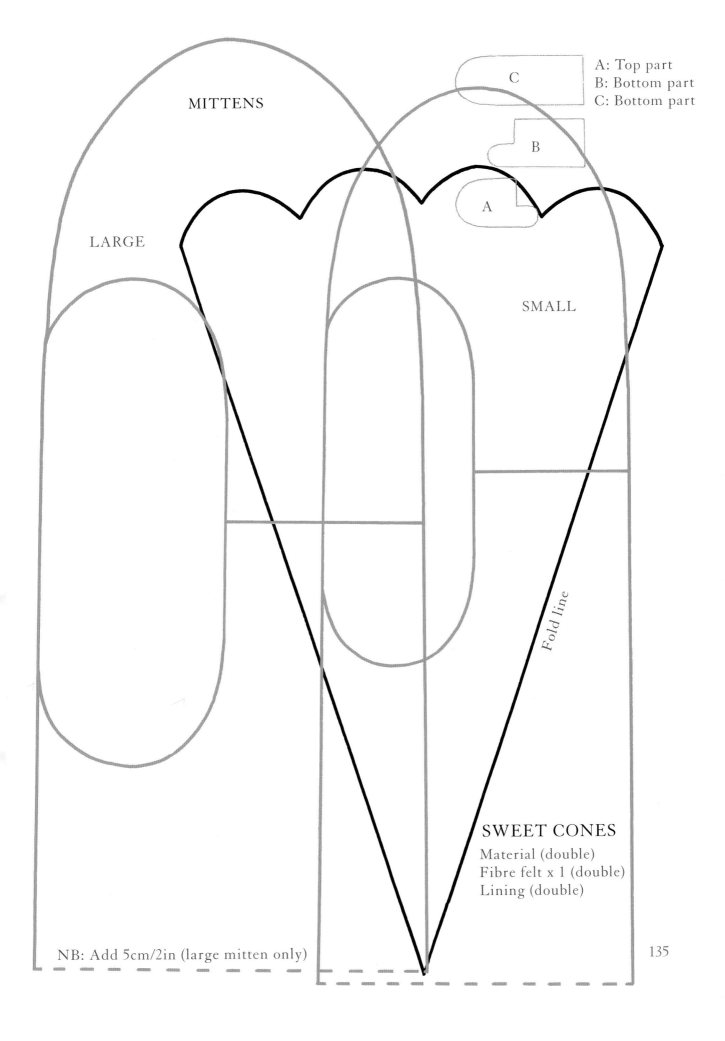

MITTENS

LARGE

SMALL

A: Top part
B: Bottom part
C: Bottom part

C

B

A

Fold line

SWEET CONES
Material (double)
Fibre felt x 1 (double)
Lining (double)

NB: Add 5cm/2in (large mitten only)

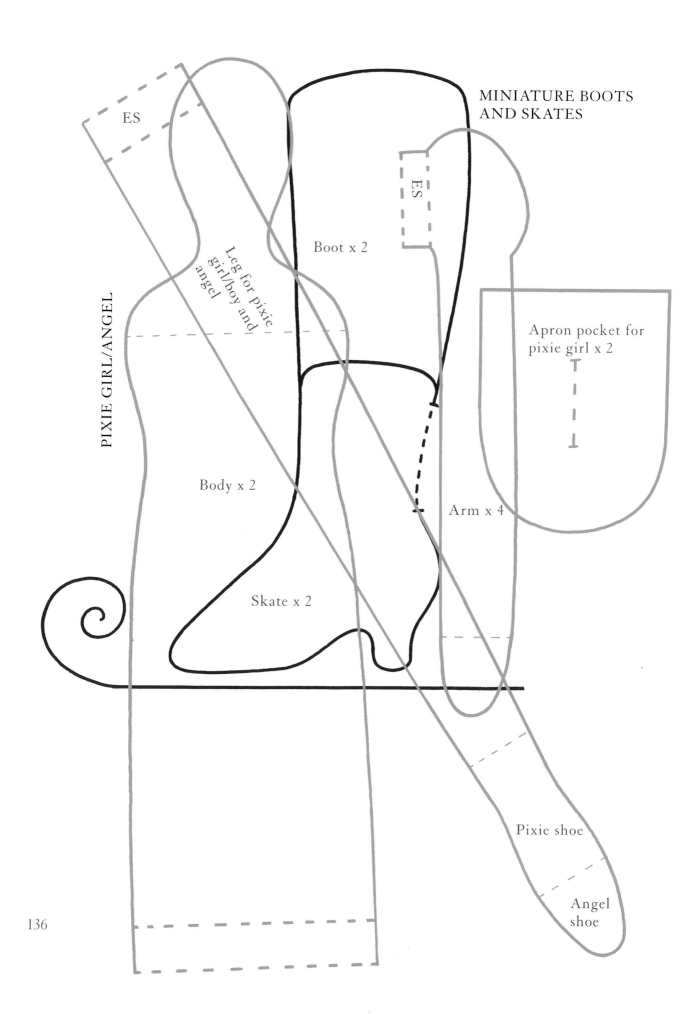

MINIATURE BOOTS
AND SKATES

ES

ES

Boot x 2

Apron pocket for
pixie girl x 2

PIXIE GIRL/ANGEL

Leg for pixie
girl/boy and
angel

Body x 2

Arm x 4

Skate x 2

Pixie shoe

Angel
shoe

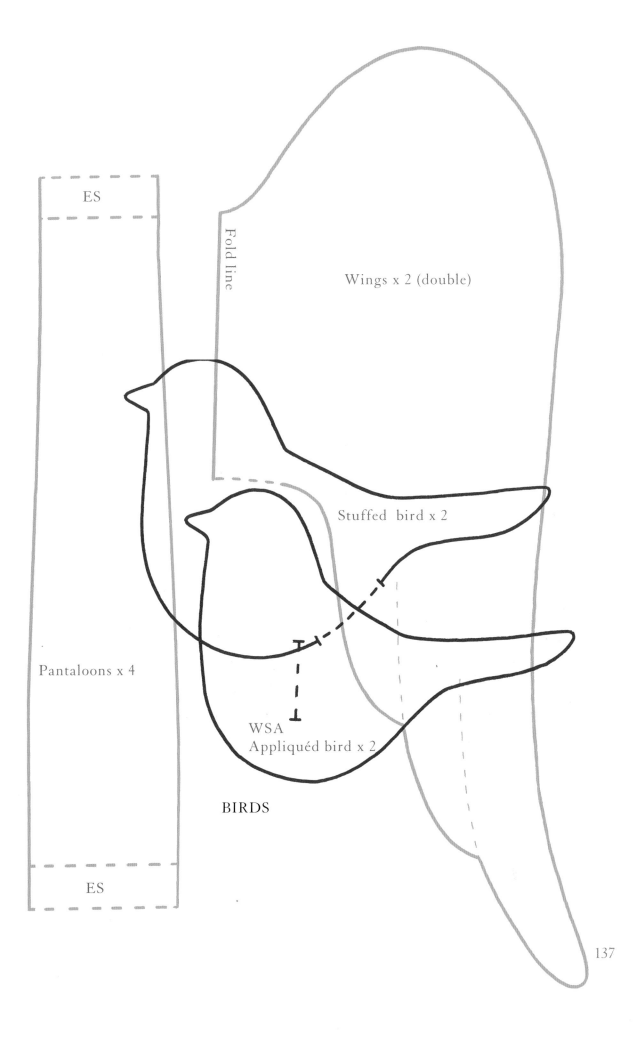

ES

Fold line

Wings x 2 (double)

Pantaloons x 4

Stuffed bird x 2

WSA
Appliquéd bird x 2

BIRDS

ES

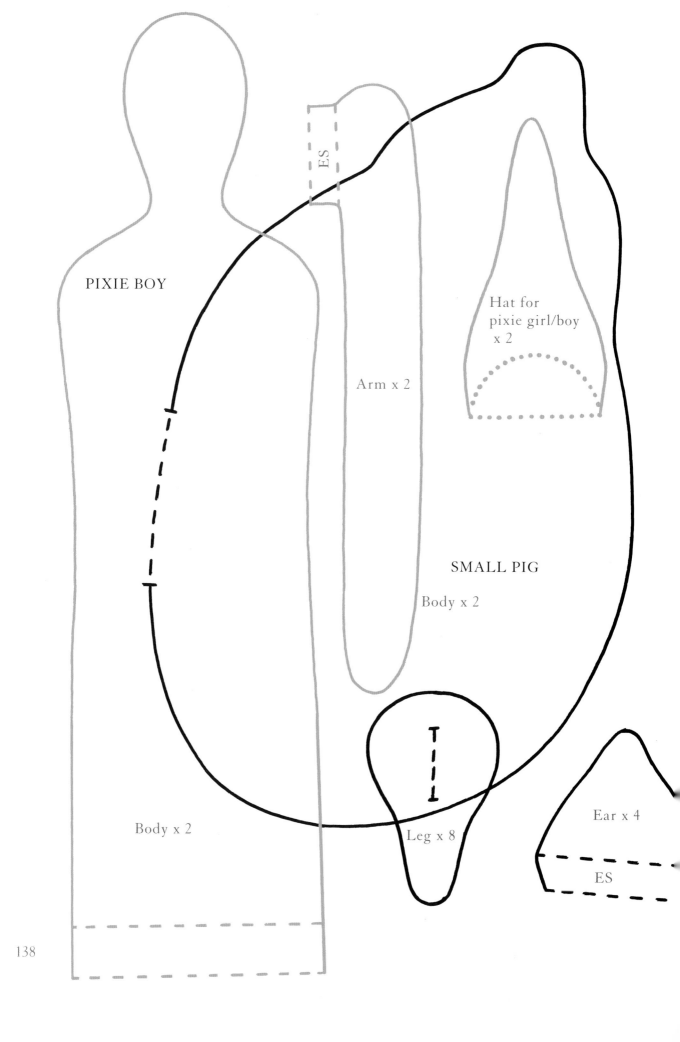

PIXIE BOY

ES

Arm x 2

Hat for
pixie girl/boy
x 2

SMALL PIG

Body x 2

Body x 2

Leg x 8

Ear x 4

ES

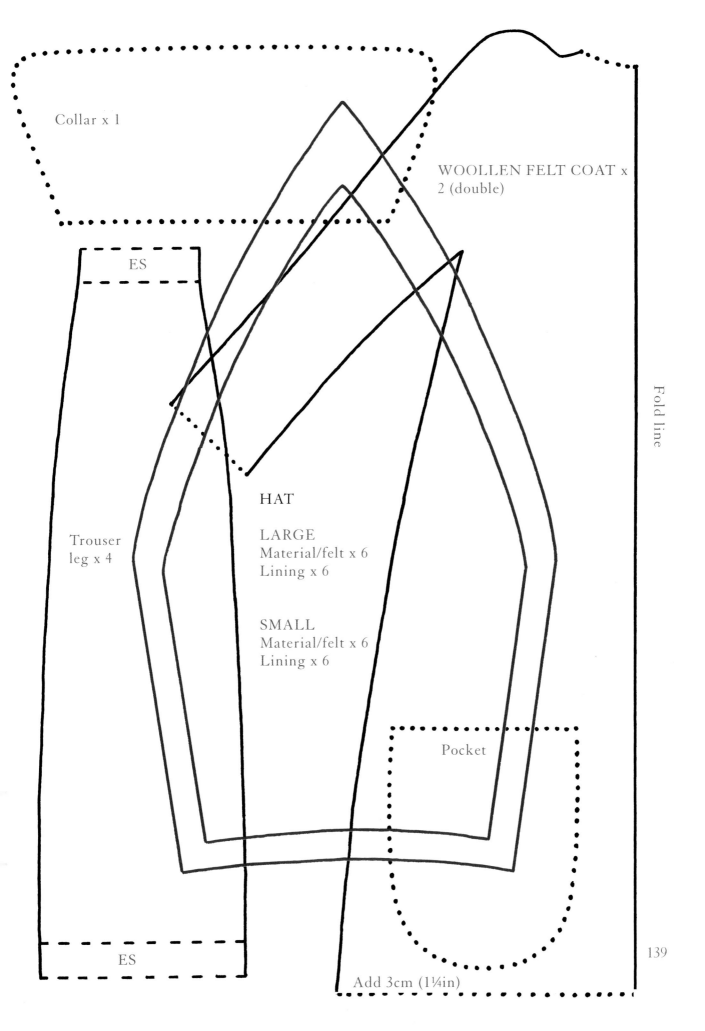

Collar x 1

WOOLLEN FELT COAT x
2 (double)

ES

Trouser
leg x 4

HAT

LARGE
Material/felt x 6
Lining x 6

SMALL
Material/felt x 6
Lining x 6

Pocket

ES

Add 3cm (1¼in)

Fold line

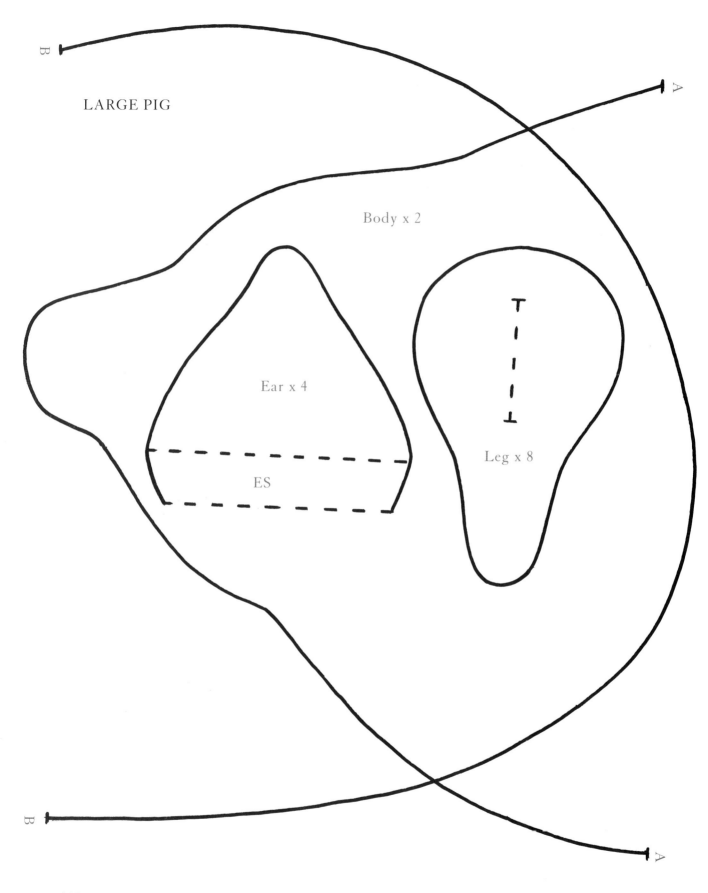

LARGE PIG

Body x 2

Ear x 4

ES

Leg x 8

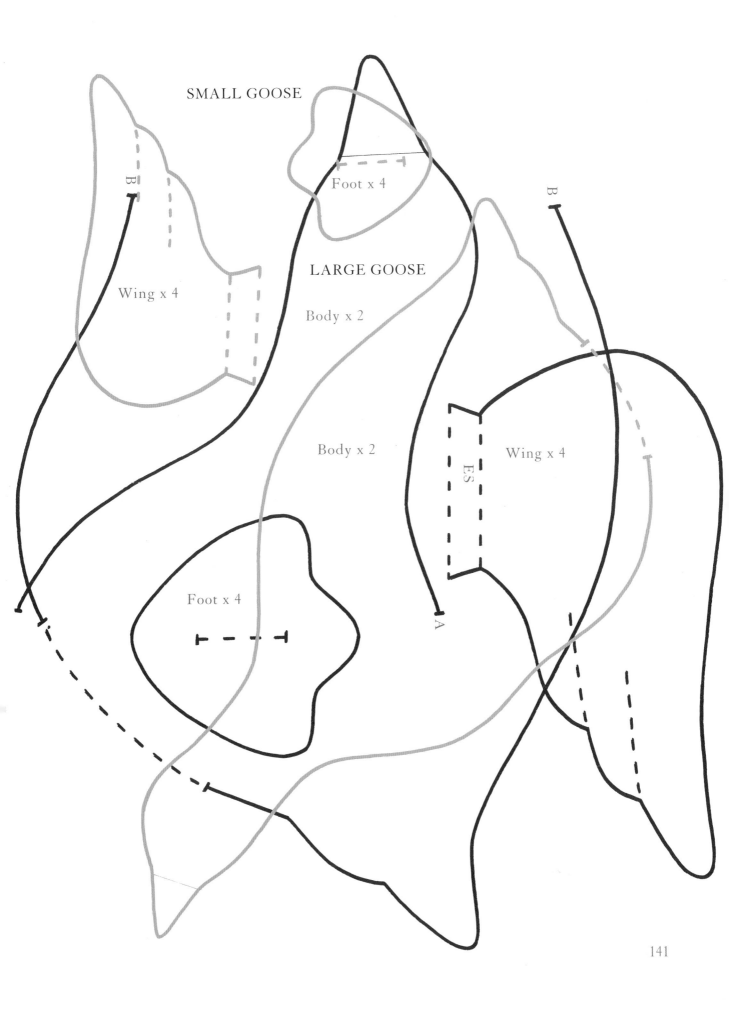

SMALL GOOSE

Foot x 4

LARGE GOOSE

Wing x 4

Body x 2

B

Body x 2

B

Wing x 4

ES

Foot x 4

A

141

MUFFIN

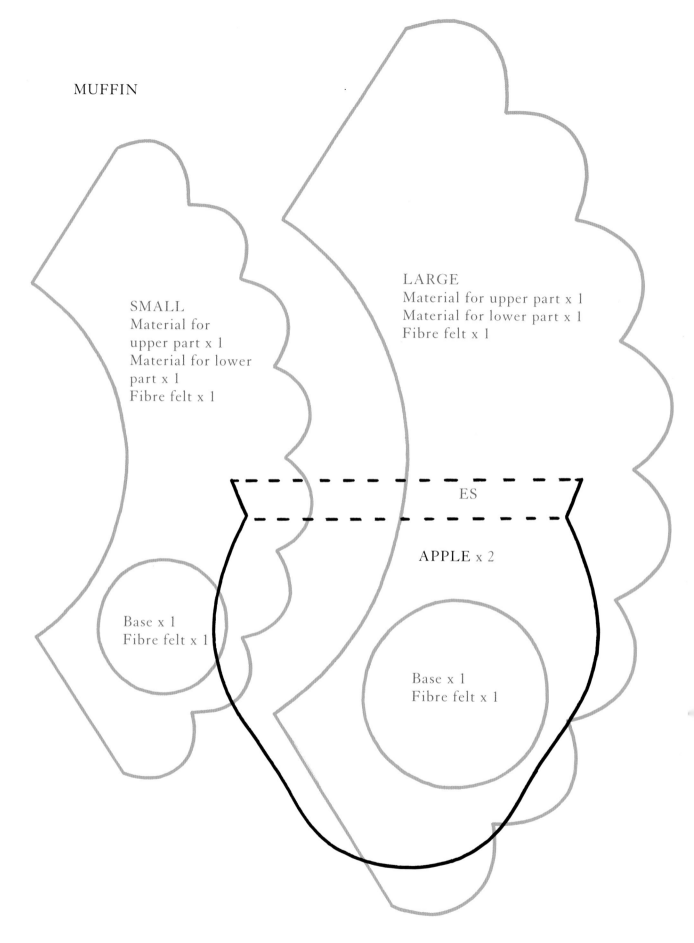

SMALL
Material for
upper part x 1
Material for lower
part x 1
Fibre felt x 1

LARGE
Material for upper part x 1
Material for lower part x 1
Fibre felt x 1

ES

APPLE x 2

Base x 1
Fibre felt x 1

Base x 1
Fibre felt x 1

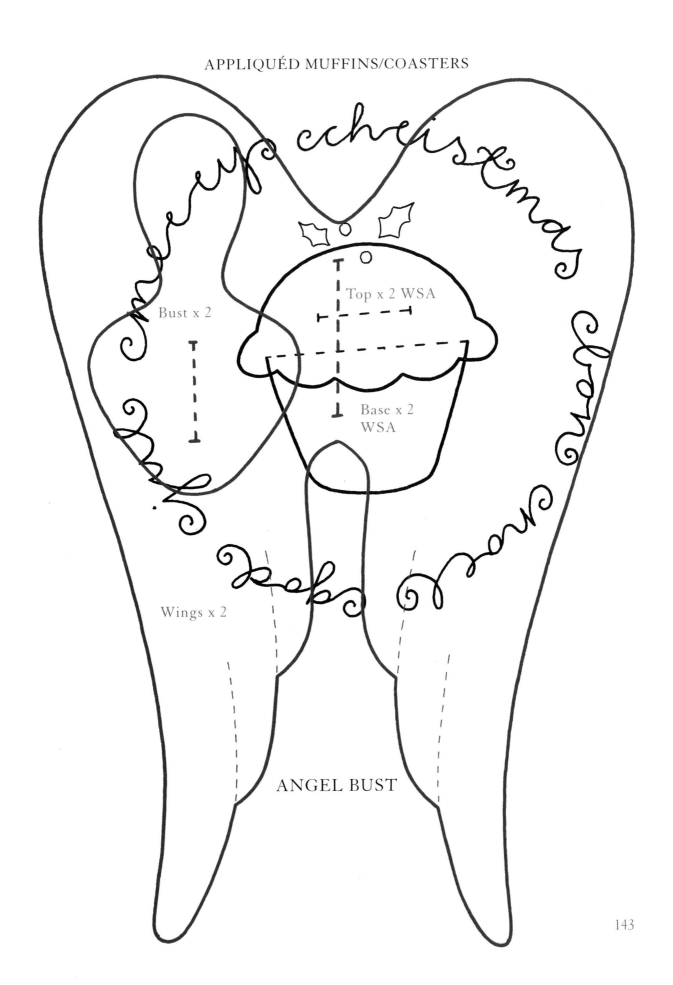

merry christmas darling merry

Bust x 2

Top x 2 WSA

Base x 2 WSA

Wings x 2

ANGEL BUST

APPLIQUÉD ANGEL BUST

WSA

Wings x 4

WSA
Bust x 2

WSA
Top x 2

ANGEL BUST TAPESTRY

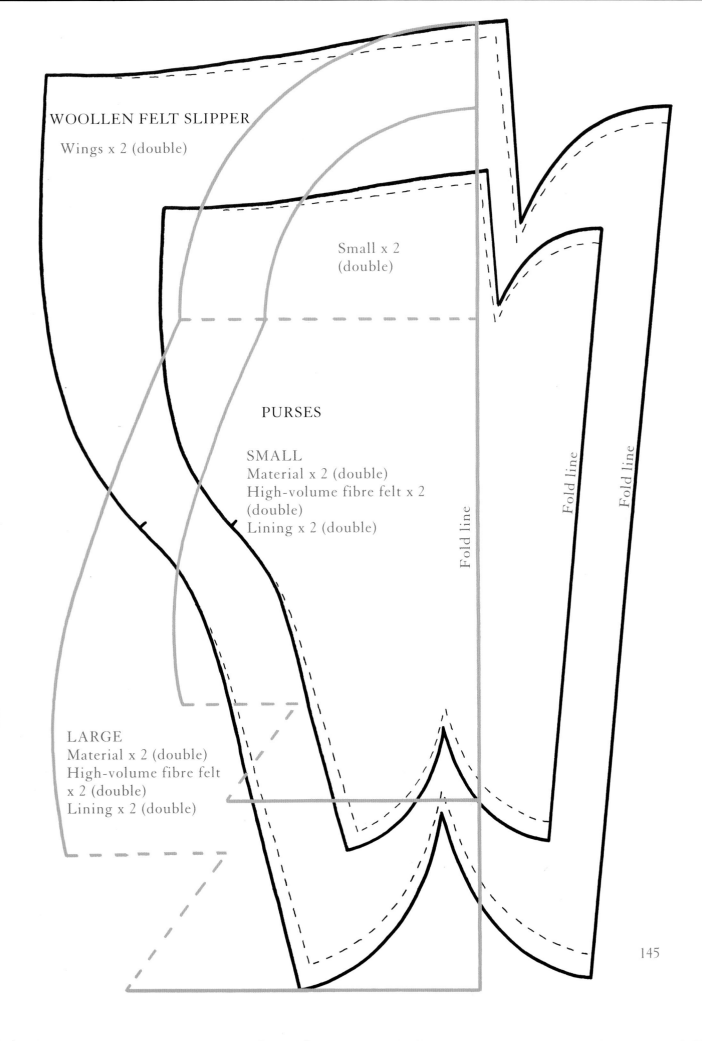

WOOLLEN FELT SLIPPER

Wings x 2 (double)

Small x 2
(double)

PURSES

SMALL
Material x 2 (double)
High-volume fibre felt x 2
(double)
Lining x 2 (double)

LARGE
Material x 2 (double)
High-volume fibre felt
x 2 (double)
Lining x 2 (double)

Fold line

Fold line

Fold line

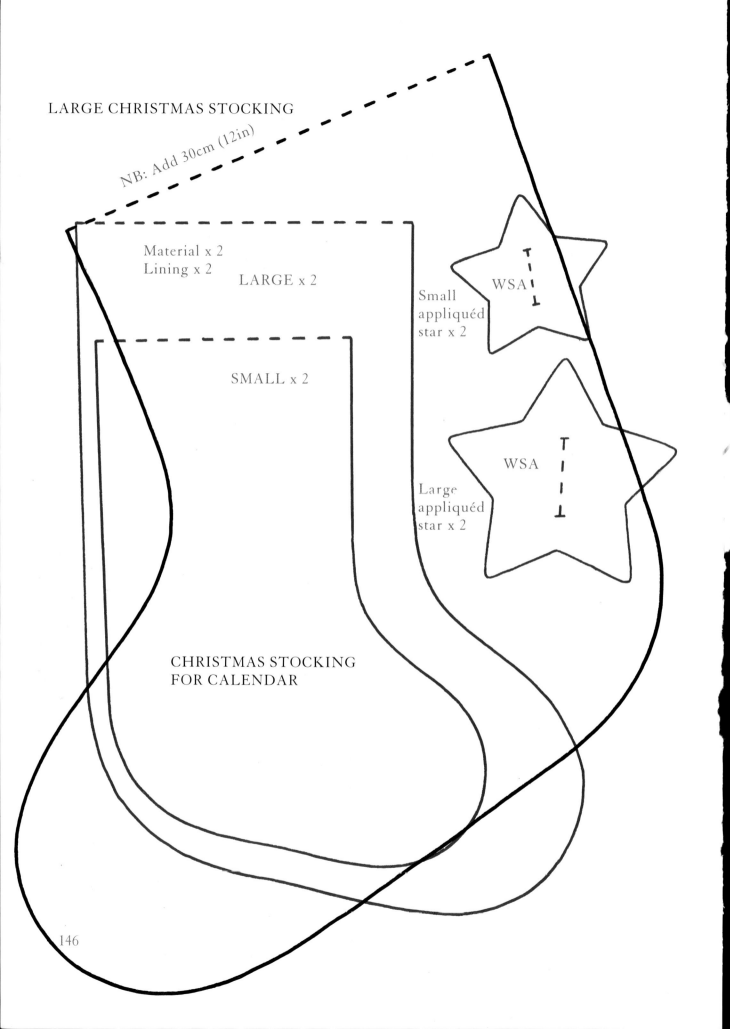

LARGE CHRISTMAS STOCKING

NB: Add 30cm (12in)

Material x 2
Lining x 2

LARGE x 2

SMALL x 2

CHRISTMAS STOCKING
FOR CALENDAR

Small
appliquéd
star x 2

WSA

Large
appliquéd
star x 2

WSA

146

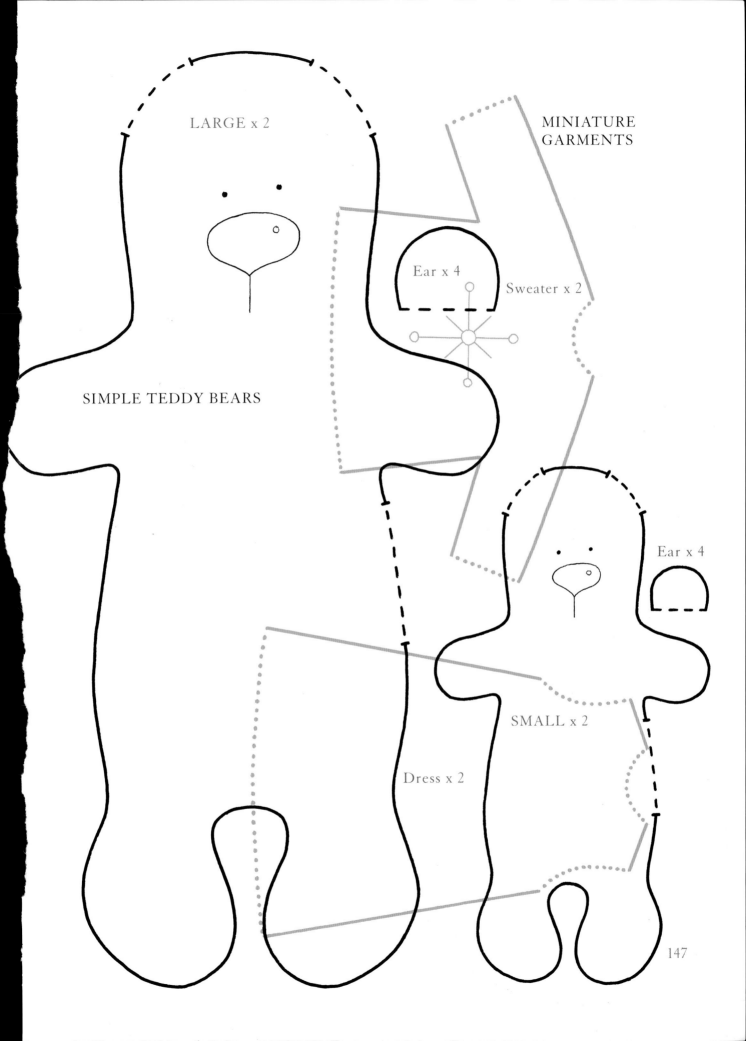

LARGE x 2

MINIATURE
GARMENTS

SIMPLE TEDDY BEARS

Ear x 4

Sweater x 2

Ear x 4

SMALL x 2

Dress x 2

147

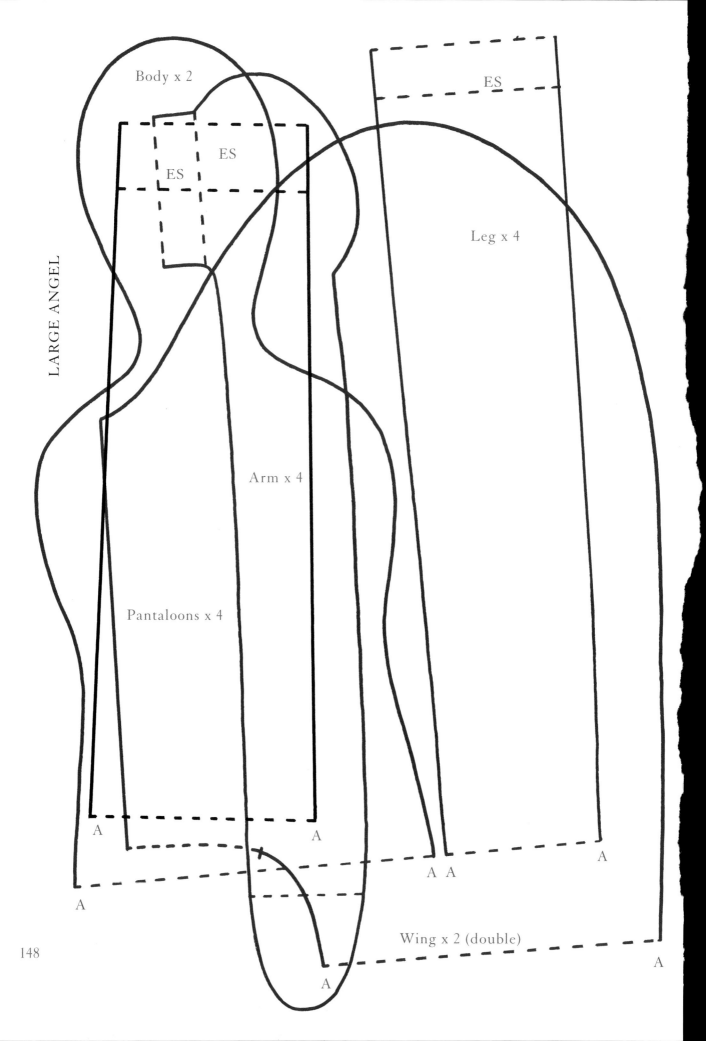

LARGE ANGEL

Body x 2

ES

ES

ES

Leg x 4

Arm x 4

Pantaloons x 4

A

A

A

A

A A

A

A

Wing x 2 (double)

A

A

148

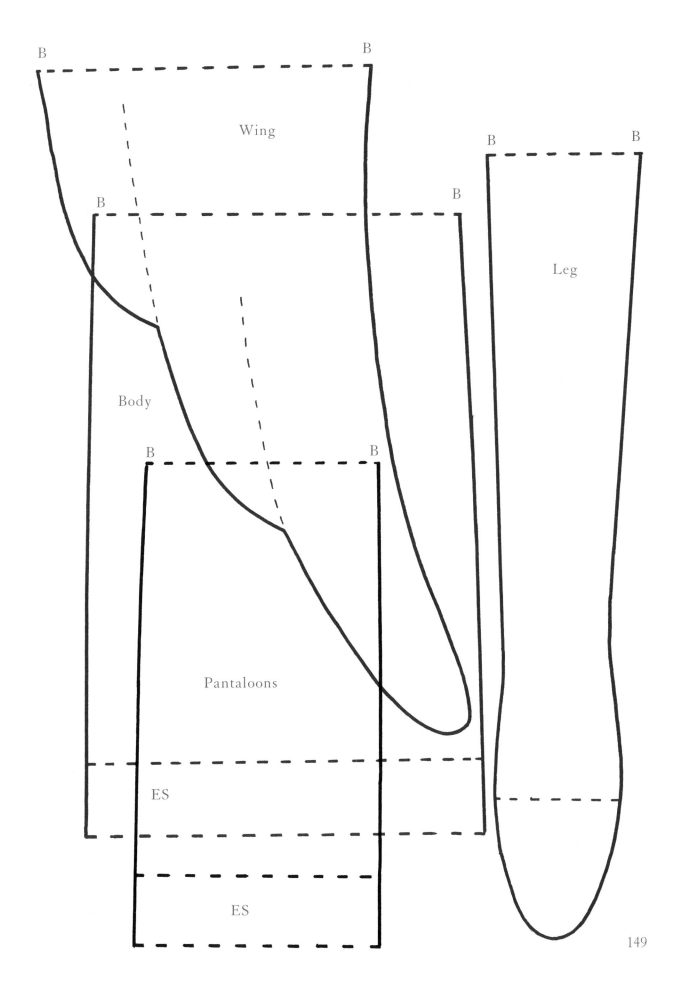

B   B

Wing

B   B

B   B

Leg

Body

B   B

Pantaloons

ES

ES

149

HOBBY REINDEER

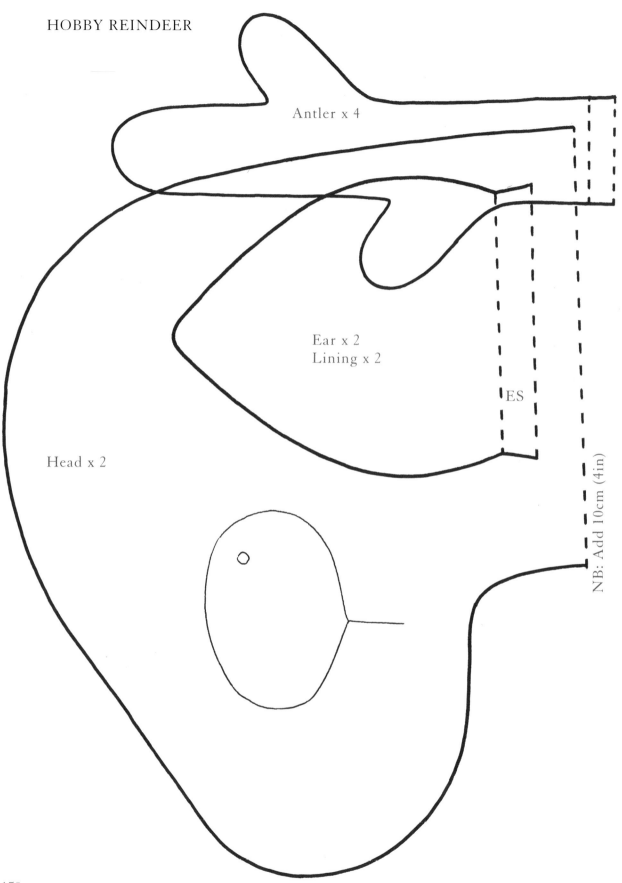

Antler x 4

Ear x 2
Lining x 2

Head x 2

ES

NB: Add 10cm (4in)

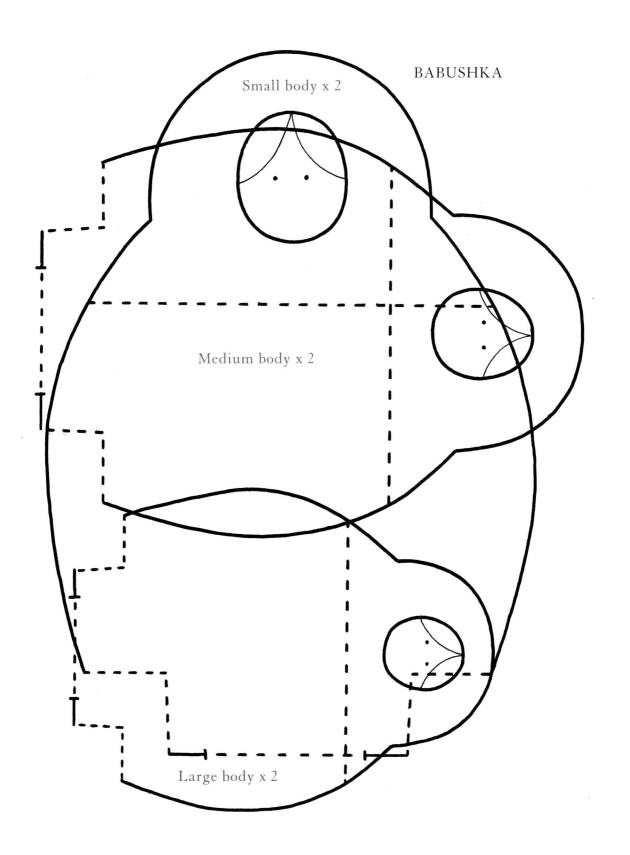

Small body x 2

Medium body x 2

Large body x 2

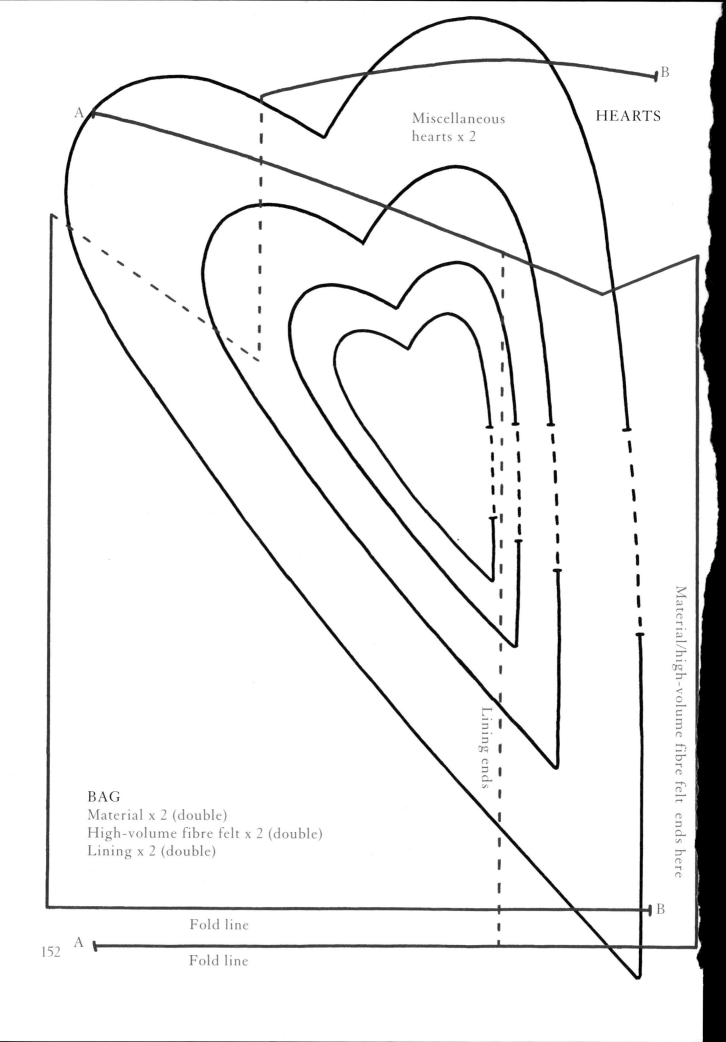

A

B

Miscellaneous
hearts x 2

HEARTS

Lining ends

Material/high-volume fibre felt ends here

BAG
Material x 2 (double)
High-volume fibre felt x 2 (double)
Lining x 2 (double)

B

Fold line

A

Fold line